IN THE
BIG
INNING

IN THE
BIG
INNING

GOOD, CLEAN
SPORTS JOKES
FOR KIDS!

SHILOH ♪ kidz
An Imprint of Barbour Publishing, Inc.

Published by Shiloh Kidz, an imprint of Barbour Publishing, Inc., 1810 Barbour Drive, Uhrichsville, Ohio 44683, www.shilohkidz.com

Our mission is to inspire the world with the life-changing message of the Bible.

Member of the
Evangelical Christian
Publishers Association

Printed in the United States of America.

000343 0520 BP

CONTENTS

INTRODUCTION

Where do you find baseball in the Bible?
Right in Genesis 1:1—*"In the big inning. . ."*

....

Yeah, that joke's been around a while. Maybe
not quite since God created the heavens and
the earth, but probably as long as baseball
has existed.

In the pages that follow, you'll find some
other oldies-but-goodies. . .maybe some
oldies-and-groanies. . .perhaps even some
newies-and-goodies. They all relate to the
sports and leisure-time activities that we
human beings love to play or watch:

- baseball, basketball, and football
- bowling, fishing, and golf
- soccer, swimming, tennis, and jai alai

Well, people play and watch jai alai, but we
don't actually have any jokes for that game.
(Apparently, it's pretty serious stuff.) All the
others, though, we'll have some fun with.

Get ready to smile, snicker, guffaw, or
groan as we throw out the first pitch of *In the
Big Inning: Good, Clean Sports Jokes for Kids!*

BASEBALL

When God said, "Let there be light,"
He started a string of events that would
lead to the first major league night game
in Cincinnati, Ohio, on May 24, 1935.
Just thought you'd like to know.

....

Baseball One-Liners

I was watching a baseball game on television
when my mom said, "Speaking of high and
outside, the grass needs mowing."

That pro doesn't steal bases—he buys them.

He's such a tough hitter he even gets walks at
batting practice.

Baseball will outlast all other sports because a
diamond is forever.

Little League

No wonder kids are so confused these days.
A Little League coach told his player, "Hold at
third," while his mother was yelling, "Johnny,
you come home this instant!"

Face-Hitter

A player threw a baseball as hard as he could. There was nothing behind him, in front of him, or on his left or right, but the ball still came back and hit him right in the face. How did that happen?

He threw it straight up in the air.

The Greatest!

A little boy was talking to himself as he strutted through the backyard carrying a ball and bat. "I'm the greatest hitter in the world!" he said. Then he tossed the ball into the air, swung at it, and missed.

"Strike one!" he yelled. Undaunted, he picked up the ball and repeated, "I'm the greatest hitter in the world!" When it came down, he swung again and missed. "Strike two!" he cried.

The boy paused a moment, examined the ball, spit on his hands, adjusted his hat, and repeated, "I'm the greatest hitter in the world!"

Again he tossed the ball up and swung at it. He missed. "Strike three!"

"Wow!" he exclaimed. "I'm the greatest *pitcher* in the world!"

Rookies!

A boastful first-year pitcher got the start in his team's first playoff game. Unfortunately, he walked the first five batters he faced, and the manager quickly pulled him from the game.

In the dugout, the rookie pitcher muttered to himself, "That crazy manager! He took me out when I had a no-hitter going!"

Dog-Ball

During a crucial kids' sandlot baseball game, a spectator was surprised to see a dog walk out to the pitcher's mound, wind up, and strike out the other all-star team. Later, he would slam two home runs.

"That's incredible," the spectator exclaimed to the man sitting next to him.

"Yes," the man said, "but he's terrible disappointment to his parents. They wanted him to play football."

Good Manners

"Look, Billy," the coach said, "you know the principles of good sportsmanship. You know the Little League doesn't allow temper tantrums, shouting at the umpire, or abusive language."

"Yes sir, I understand."

"Good, Billy. Now, would you please explain that to your mother?"

A Really Bad Batter

He doesn't have a good sense of the strike zone. He once swung at a pick-off throw to first base.

Winning Run

Coming home from his Little League game, Bud excitedly swung open the front door and hollered, "Anyone home?"

His father immediately asked, "So how did you do, son?"

"You'll never believe it!" Buddy announced. "I was responsible for the winning run!"

"Really? How'd you do that?"

"I dropped the ball."

Control

A rookie pitcher was struggling at the mound, causing the catcher to walk up to have a talk. "I've figured out your problem," he told the pitcher. "You always lose control at the same point in every game."

"When is that?"

"Right after the National Anthem."

Can't Fool That Kid!

The sixth-grade teacher was leading a class on American geography. She wanted the students to learn which cities belonged to certain states, so she asked, "Does anyone know where Cleveland is?"

Ben raised his hand and shouted, "Ohio!"

"Good, Ben. Now can anyone tell me where Philadelphia is?"

"Pennsylvania!" Sarah said eagerly.

"That's right," the teacher replied, smiling. Then she tried to trick the students by asking, "And where is Kansas City?"

Charles popped up, saying "I know! I know!"

"All right, Charles," the teacher said. "Where is Kansas City?"

"In last place!"

Just Horsing Around

A baseball scout heard an unbelievable story about a horse that could hit a baseball. He couldn't imagine it was true, but out of curiosity, went down to the farm to see what he would find.

Sure enough, the horse was swinging a bat and whacking the ball far into the meadow. The scout arranged a major league tryout for the big hitter.

In the stadium, the horse slammed the first pitch he hit over the centerfield fence. The manager was impressed, but wanted to see the horse run the bases too. "Run!" he shouted.

"Run?" the horse repeated. "If I could run, I'd be in the Kentucky Derby!"

Baseball Date

It was only her second date with a diehard baseball fan, and Judy was a little nervous. It was her fault they arrived at the ballpark a full hour after the game had started.

Taking her seat, Judy glanced up at the scoreboard. It was a tight pitcher's battle, bottom of the fifth, 0–0. "Look, Charlie," she exclaimed with relief, "we haven't missed a thing."

Playing Hooky

He had hoped the situation would improve,

but finally the boss was compelled to call Andy into his office. "It has not escaped my attention," he began, "that every time there's a home baseball game, you have to take your mom to the doctor."

"Really?" asked Andy. "Come to think of it, you're right, sir. I didn't realize it. You don't suppose she's faking it, do you?"

Keep Running!

"I don't understand you, Skeets," said the Little League coach to one of his slower players. "The distance between first and second base is exactly the same as the distance between second and third. Why does it take you longer to reach third?"

"Well, Coach," answered Skeets, "everyone knows there's a short stop between second and third."

The Golden State

"I really like playing ball in San Jo-see," said the minor league player to his roommate.

"Hank, here in California there are lots of Spanish names," his roommate interrupted. "The natives pronounce the letter *J* as an *H*. We say 'San Hosay.' "

"Hmm."

"By the way, when do we play there again?"

"In Hune and Huly."

Answer Me This

Why do people sing "Take Me Out to the Ball Game" when they're already there?

$how Me the Money

What do you call forty millionaires sitting around watching the World Series?

The New York Yankees.

Surprise Game

Two old men, named Frank and Saul, sat on a park bench talking, and the conversation turned to baseball. Frank asked Saul, "Do you think there's baseball in heaven?"

Saul thought for a moment and replied, "I don't know. But let's make a deal. If I get there first, I'll somehow get word to you and tell you if there's baseball in heaven. If you die first, you need to promise to do the same." They shook on it and didn't speak of it again.

Unfortunately, a few months later, Frank

passed away. Saul soon returned to the park bench daily where he and his friend had spent so many hours talking together. One day, he began to doze off and heard what sounded like Frank's voice. "Frank, is that you?" asked Saul in a shaky voice.

"Yes, it is, Saul," he heard. Saul, stunned, said, "So, is there baseball in heaven?"

"Well, I have good news and bad news," Frank answered.

"Give me the good news first," Saul said.

"Okay. Yes, there is baseball in heaven," Frank admitted.

Saul exclaimed, "That's wonderful! What could ever be bad news?"

Frank paused then said, "You're pitching on Tuesday."

Q & A

Q: Why did the baseball player go to jail?
A: Because he was caught trying to steal second base!

Q: Why does it get hot after a baseball game?
A: Because all the fans leave.

Q: Why did the baseball player take his bat to the library?

A: Because his teacher told him to hit the books.

Q: What do you call a baseball with bugs on it?

A: A fly ball.

Q: Why didn't the first baseman get to dance with Cinderella?

A: He missed the ball.

Q: Do baseball players text each other often?

A: Not really, but they do touch base every once in a while.

Q: Which singers make the best baseball players?

A: The ones with perfect pitch.

Q: You are locked inside the car with only a baseball bat. How do you get out?

A: Unlock the door!

Q: Why don't matches play baseball?

A: One strike and they're out.

Stealing Base

What is the best kind of shoes to wear for stealing bases?

Sneakers.

Umpire-Itis

Fred is a minor-league umpire. He's used to being heckled by fans. But he really got a surprise at a particular exhibition game. After a long search for a place to change clothes, Fred finally located a room with a neatly lettered sign: Umpires' Dressing Room.

As he was about to go in, however, he inspected the sign more closely. Below the printed ID was the same message—in Braille.

Kind of Scary

A man leaves home, makes three left turns, and returns home, where two masked men are waiting for him. Who are they?

The catcher and the umpire.

Yogi Berra Quotes

"If the people don't want to come out to the ballpark, nobody's gonna stop them."

"No wonder nobody comes here; it's too crowded."

"We make too many wrong mistakes."

Play Time

Logan knocked on the front door of his friend Burt's house. When the mother of the boy answered the door, Logan asked, "Can Burt come out to play?"

"No," answered the mother, "it's too cold."

"Well then," said Logan, "can his ball glove come out to play?"

Good Pitching

Toby: What would you get if you crossed a baseball player with a Boy Scout?

Jack: I don't know, but I bet he could sure pitch a tent!

It's Not Goodbye

What did the outfielder's glove say to the baseball?

"Catch you later!"

Look Out!

Dad: What happened to your eye?
Kevin: I was staring at a ball from afar, and I
was wondering why it was getting
bigger and bigger. Then, it hit me.

Riddle Roundup

Why are frogs such good baseball players?
They love to catch flies.

Who is Count Dracula's favorite person on
the team?
The bat boy.

Where is the largest diamond in the world?
On a baseball field.

What is the best way to get rid of flies?
Sign up some good outfielders.

What runs around a baseball field but never
moves?
The fence.

What happened when the Invisible Man
pitched at the game?
There was pitching like you have never seen.

Why was night baseball started?
Because all bats like to sleep in the daytime.

What team cries when it loses?
A bawl club.

Why couldn't the skeleton play baseball?
His heart just wasn't in it.

How did the baseball player lose his house?
He made his home run.

What has eighteen legs and catches flies?
A baseball team.

How is a baseball team like a cake?
They both need a good batter.

Would chickens make good umpires?
No—they always call fowl balls.

Have you heard the joke about the pop fly?
Probably not. It's over your head.

What does an umpire do before he eats?
He brushes off his plate.

What is the best day to play a doubleheader?
Twos-day.

Where is the headquarters for the Umpire's Association?

The Umpire State Building.

Two baseball teams played a game. One team won, but no man touched base. How could that be?

Both were all-girl teams.

What do four balls mean in baseball?

It means you can lose three and still be okay.

What can you catch but not throw?

A cold.

Which baseball player carries the water?

The pitcher, of course.

BASKETBALL

There are plenty of baskets in the Bible, from the one baby Moses floated in to the ones the disciples used to pick up the leftovers after Jesus fed five thousand people with one kid's lunch. There's even a ball in scripture—check out Isaiah 22:18. But there's just no basketball in the Bible. You'll have to be content with the jokes that follow.

....

Ref Riff

The captain of a basketball team says to the referee, "My coach wants to know if there is a penalty for thinking."

The ref says, "No."

The captain says, "Well, my coach thinks you're awful!"

Final Exam

Two college basketball players were taking an important exam. If they failed, they would not be allowed to play in the big game the following week. The exam was fill-in-the-blanks. The last question read, "Old Mac-Donald had a _____."

Bubba was stumped. He had no idea how to answer, but he knew he needed this answer to play in the big game next week. So he tapped Tiny on the shoulder and asked for the answer to the last question.

Tiny carefully turned around to Bubba and said, "Bubba, you don't know this? Everyone knows Old MacDonald had a *farm*."

"Oh yeah," said Bubba. "I remember now." After a long pause, he tapped Tiny on the shoulder and whispered, "Tiny, how do you spell farm?"

Tiny just rolled his eyes. "That's so easy. *Farm* is spelled E-I-E-I-O."

Knock, Knock

Knock, knock.
    Who's there?
Tijuana.
    Tijuana who?
Tijuana shoot some hoops later?

Pay-Off

Basketball is supposed to build bodies. That's funny! I watched four games this weekend, and I don't look any different.

Man Called "Joe"

A basketball player named Joe made a terrible mistake. He robbed a convenience store in his own neighborhood. The owner of the store instantly recognized the six-foot, seven-inch hoops star, despite his pathetic attempt to wear a mask. When the owner said, "Joe, don't do this, okay?" the masked man replied, "No, it ain't me. It ain't me."

Putting Up with Jocks

The basketball coach stormed into the university president's office and demanded a raise right there and then.

"Please," protested the college president, "you already make more than the entire history department."

"Yeah, maybe so, but you don't know what I have put up with," the coach fumed. "Look."

He went out into the hall and grabbed a player who was jogging down the hallway. "Run over to my office and see if I'm there," he ordered.

Twenty minutes later, the young man returned, sweaty and out of breath. "You're not there, sir," he reported.

"Oh, I see what you mean," conceded the president, scratching his head. "*I* would have phoned."

Q & A

Q: Why did the chicken cross the basketball court?
A: Because it heard the referee calling fouls.

Q: Why do basketball players like to eat doughnuts?
A: Because they can dunk them.

Q: Why are spiders the best basketball players?
A: Because they are all eight-footers.

Q: Why did the basketball player always bring his suitcase to the games?
A: He was known for traveling a lot.

Q: What kind of stories do basketball players tell?
A: Tall tales.

Q: What did March say in the middle of the madness?
A: What's all the bracket?

Misquotes

A college basketball coach was talking to a player who received four Fs and one D. "Son," he said, "it looks to me like you're spending too much time on one subject."

The Interview

"He's really great on the court," a sportswriter said of a college basketball player in an interview with his coach. "But how's his scholastic record?"

"Why, he makes straight A's," replied the coach.

"Wonderful!" said the sportswriter.

"Yes," agreed the coach, "but his B's are a little crooked."

Trophy Case Mystery

At Central High School, the trophy case contained photos of all the previous basket-ball teams. In each photo, the player in the center held a ball labeled with the season: 81–82, 82–83, 83–84, and so on. One day after practice, a freshman player was inspecting the old pictures. "Hey Coach," he called out, "isn't it strange how every one of these teams lost by a single point?"

Never Fails

Whenever I go to a ball game, I always end up in the same seat—between the hot dog vendor and his best customer.

Murphy's Laws of Spectator Sports: Exciting plays occur only while you are out buying french fries.

Actual Hoopster Quotes

A senior player at the University of Pittsburgh: "I'm going to graduate on time no matter how long it takes."

A coach once demanded, "You guys line up alphabetically by height," and "You guys pair up in groups of three, and then line up in a circle."

A certain Orlando general manager, discussing his team's 7–27 record: "We can't win at home. We can't win on the road. I just can't figure out where else to play."

One-Liners

Our center's not very bright. I think he's banged his head on too many doorways.

He's such a versatile player he can do any-thing wrong.

He's so tall he looks like a flagpole with hair.

We have so many injuries, the team picture is an X-ray.

I won't say he's overweight, but his stomach crosses midcourt three steps before he does.

Riddle Roundup

Why can't you play basketball with pigs?
Because they're likely to hog the ball.

Why are babies good at basketball?
Because they dribble well.

What do basketball players do when their eyesight goes bad?
Become referees.

Which basketball player wears the biggest shoes?
The one with the biggest feet.

BOATING

Now, *here's* a topic with a definite
Bible connection! There are boats
all through the Bible, from Noah's
great big ark to the ship that sank under
the apostle Paul. Speaking of sinking. . .

....

It Just Takes Once. . .

A crew member was nervous his first time
onboard. He asked the skipper, "Do boats like
this sink very often?"

"Not too often," answered the skipper.
"Usually it's only once."

Punny

Two Eskimos sitting in a kayak were chilly, but
when they lit a fire in the boat, it sank, proving once more than you can't have your kayak
and heat it too.

Dentist's Boat

A dentist opened an office on a boat. What
was the boat's name?

The Tooth Ferry.

New Business

A woman opened a new business in her home supplying parts for sailboats. Her sails went through the roof.

Funny Boat Names

Pier Pressure
Moor Often Than Knot
To Sea or Not to Sea
Seas the Day

Knock, Knock

Knock, knock.
   Who's there?
Canoe.
   Canoe who?
Canoe come over and play?

Light Signals

Peering out into the pitch-black night, a sea captain spots a light straight ahead. It's on a collision course with his ship. He sends out a light signal: "Change your course fifteen degrees west."

The light immediately signals back to the

ship, "Change your course fifteen degrees east."

The captain became angry. He replies with a second signal declaring, "I'm a navy captain! Change your course!"

"I'm a seaman, second class," comes back in reply. "You change your course, sir."

The captain is now irate. "I am a battle-ship!" he signals. "I am not changing course."

He receives one final call, stating, "I am a lighthouse. It's your call."

Boating Quip

Did you hear about the big fight over paddles at the sporting goods store? It was a huge oar deal!

Riddle Roundup

What happened when a Red team's boat crashed into the Blue team's boat?

The crew was marooned.

Why do scuba divers fall backward out of the boat?

Because if they fell forward, they would fall into the boat.

What detergent do sailors use?
Tide.

What is the best thing to give a boat if it isn't well?
Vitamin sea.

What do you call a boat full of polite athletes?
A good sportsman ship.

What do you do with a sick boat?
Take it to the doc.

How do competing boating teams greet each other?
They wave.

Why did the sailor ask his captain to look at a boat he was considering purchasing?
Because it never hurts to have an extra aye.

BOWLING

You know, if Goliath had challenged David to a few frames of bowling instead of that "come out and fight me" business, things might not have turned out so badly for him. Just sayin'. . .

....

Realistic Rule Addition

After a member of the opposing team bowls four strikes in a row, he or she must bowl the next four frames blindfolded. If he or she continues to strike, his or her shoelaces will be tied together for two frames.

Veggie Bowl

A bowler whose game has fallen off lately walks into a psychiatrist's office with a cucumber up his nose, a carrot in his left ear, and a banana in his right ear. "What's the matter with me?"

With great insight, the doctor says, "You're not eating properly."

Trick Play

He was a professional bowler before he became a power basketball forward. You should see his "alley-hoop" play.

Team Bowling

Two bowling teams charter a double-decker bus for a weekend bowling tournament in Atlantic City. The Green team rode on the bottom of the bus while the Orange team perched on the top level.

As the bus weaves through traffic and visits all the sightseeing points, Green team below is having a great time. Everyone is whooping it up, when someone suddenly realizes nothing can be heard from the Orange's level. Dashing up the stairs, a team member from below finds all the Orange team sitting frozen with fear, staring straight ahead with white knuckles.

The Green team representative asks, "What's the trouble up here? We're having a grand time downstairs." One of the Orange team members looks up and says, "Well sure, *you* have a driver!"

Short Takes

Bowling is a sport that should be right down your alley.

"Something's wrong with my bowling delivery," Tom said gutterally.

If you can't hear a pin drop, something is obviously wrong with your bowling.

Punny

Evidence has been discovered that shows William Tell and his family enjoyed bowling. Unfortunately, all of the official records were destroyed in a fire, and so we will never truly know for whom the Tells bowled.

Riddle Roundup

Why should football players not go bowling?
They tend to spike the ball.

What does a bowler and a family Thanksgiving have in common?
They both look forward to a turkey (in bowling, 3 strikes in a row).

Why is bowling easier than golfing?
It's more difficult to lose a bowling ball.

Where is Superman's favorite place to bowl?
Lois Lanes.

What is the quietest sport?
Bowling, because you can hear a pin drop.

Why are good bowlers sometimes not the best employees?
Because they strike a lot.

What kind of dog hangs around bowling alleys?
A setter.

Why do good bowlers play so slowly?
Because they have time to spare.

What can you do with old bowling balls?
Give them to elephants for shooting marbles.

Why did the bowling pins stop working?
They went on strike.

BOXING

No joke—the apostle Paul referred to boxing in 1 Corinthians 9:26: "I do not fight like a boxer beating the air." He meant he was serious about following Jesus. You should be too. . .but you can still enjoy the following boxing jokes:

....

Q & A

Q: Does a match box?
A: No, but a tin can!

Q: How do you make a fruit punch?
A: Give it boxing lessons.

Q: What do they call the boxer who gets beaten up by the heavyweight champion?
A: A sore loser.

Q: Why didn't the dog want to play baseball?
A: Because it's a boxer.

Talkin' Boxin'

"Coach, my sparring partner called in sick. Can I train alone today?"
    "Knock yourself out."

A man purchased a gift and the cashier said, "Do you wanna box for that?"

The boxer sighed and said, "Can't we settle this peacefully?"

He was a crossword puzzle boxer. You know, he entered the ring vertical and left it horizontal.

On a boxer's tombstone: YOU CAN STOP COUNTING. I'M NOT GETTING UP.

Boxing Ponderings

The fans were getting restless. The boxing match hadn't started yet, but it was a bout to begin.

I went to my first kick boxing class tonight—hopefully I'll be able to quit boxing for good this time.

Why is a boxing ring square?

Ouch!

A cocky young boxer told his manager, "I'm going to fight in front of millions on TV tonight!"

"Yeah," the realistic manager answered, "and they'll all know the result of the fight at least ten seconds before you do."

Ouch, Part Two!

Smith and Johnson were scheduled to box one Friday night. Halfway into the third round, Smith unleashed a powerful punch that caught Johnson square in the nose. Johnson dropped like a sack of cement to the mat, where the referee began counting.

Johnson's manager climbed into the ring to help the dazed fighter onto a stretcher. The boxer finally stirred and mumbled, "What happened? I feel awful. . . ."

"Take it easy, champ," the manager answered. "You're better off than Smith right now."

Johnson was coming around. "What do you mean?" he asked. "I never laid a glove on him."

"True," the manager replied. "But he's back there in the ring thinking he killed you!"

Riddle Roundup

What's a boxer's favorite drink?
Punch.

What is the difference between a boxer and a man with a head cold?

One knows his blows, and the other blows his nose.

What is the UPS driver's favorite sport?

Boxing.

What's the difference between a nail and the loser of a boxing match?

One gets knocked in and the other gets knocked out.

What happened when the boxer saw his reflection in the mirror?

He thought the resemblance was striking.

How did the pirate become a boxing champion?

He had a great left hook.

What is a fighter's favorite dog?

A boxer.

What kind of match can't start a fire?

A boxing match.

What did the boxer do after the fight was over?

Hit the sack.

CYCLING

In Bible times, "two wheeler" usually meant a donkey cart or a chariot. In the 1800s, somebody moved the wheels into single-file and created the bicycle. Then people started creating cycling jokes.

....

Dog Training

"I've really had it with my dog. He'll chase anyone on a bicycle."

"So what are you going to do, lock him in the backyard? Sell him?"

"No, nothing that drastic. I think I'll just take his bike away."

Hogwash

"I was bicycling down a narrow, twisting, mountain road during a training session. A woman was driving very slowly uphill, honking her horn and shouting at me, 'Pig! Pig!'

"I made a face at her and shouted back, 'Out of my way, you old cow!'

"Then I collided with the pig."

In Tandem

A country preacher, making his rounds on his bicycle, was stopped by a suspicious traffic cop. After checking the bike thoroughly but finding nothing troublesome, he was about to let the minister go.

"You will never arrest me," declared the preacher, "because God is with me wherever I go."

"Well, then," said the cop, "I'm ticketing you for carrying a passenger on a single-seat vehicle."

Extreme Riding

There was this man from Arizona who decided to ride a ten-speed bike from Phoenix to Flagstaff. He got as far as Canyon City before the mountain road became too steep and he could go no farther.

The road was empty and it was three hours before a car finally came by. A man in a Corvette pulled over and offered the biker a ride. Of course, the bike wouldn't fit in the car, so the Corvette owner found a piece of rope, then tied one end to his bumper and the other end to the bike. He told the biker that if the car got going too fast, the biker should honk his bike horn.

Everything went fine for the first thirty miles. Then, suddenly, another Corvette blew past. Not to be outdone, the driver pulling the bike took off after the other car. A short distance down the road the two Corvettes, going well over 120 miles an hour, tore through a speed trap.

The officer noted the speeds from his radar gun and radioed to another officer ahead that he had two Corvettes headed his way speeding over 120 miles per hour. "And you're not going to believe this," he added, "but there's a guy on a ten-speed bike honking to pass."

You Know You're a Serious Cycler If. . .

- You buy your crutches instead of renting them.
- You refuse to buy a couch for your living room because that stretch of wall space is taken up by your bike.
- You empathize with roadkill.
- You can tell your dad, with a straight face, that it's too warm to mow the lawn, and then push off on your bike for a marathon.

Bike Customs

A cyclist in Europe was stopped by a customs agent. "What's in the bags?" asked the officer, pointing to a load in the bike carryall.

"Sand," said the cyclist.

"Let me take a look," said the official.

The cyclist did as he was told, emptied the bags, and proved they contained nothing but sand. Then he refilled the bags, loaded them back on the bike, and continued across the border.

A week later, the same thing happened again. In fact, the process continued every week for a year, until one day the cyclist with the sandbags failed to appear.

A few months later, the customs agent saw the cyclist living it up in a downtown restaurant. "You sure had us confused," he said. "We knew you were smuggling something across the border." Looking to see if anyone was listening, the agent said, "I won't say a word, but what were you smuggling?"

The rider smiled and answered, "Bicycles!"

Tandem Hillclimb

For their twenty-fifth wedding anniversary, Bob and Sue bought themselves a tandem bicycle. On their first ride, they encountered a steep hill. But with a lot of effort, they finally reached the top.

"Wow, that was a tough climb," Bob gasped. "I wasn't sure we were going to make it all the way up."

"Yeah," Sue agreed. "I'm glad I kept the brakes on the whole time. Otherwise, we might have rolled backwards."

Gym Cycling

"Lie flat on your backs, class, and circle your feet in the air as if you were riding your bikes," said the gym teacher. "Fred! What are you doing? Why aren't you moving your feet?"

"Oh, I'm coasting."

Ouch!

Did you hear about the vampire bike that went around biting people's necks? It was a vicious cycle.

Q & A

Q: Why did the boy take his bike to bed with him?
A: He didn't want to walk in his sleep.

Q: What is the best city to go biking in?
A: Wheeling, West Virginia.

Q: Why can't a bike stand up by itself?
A: Because it's two-tired.

That Hurt!

John was racing around the neighborhood on his new bike and called out to his mother to watch his tricks:

"Look, Mom, no hands!

"Look, Mom, no feet!

"*Waaah!* Look, Mom, no teeth!"

I Guess That's Luck

A small-town guy was visiting the big city. Distracted by all the people, vehicles, and tall buildings, he stepped off the curb and right into the path of a bicyclist. The visitor was knocked flat.

The bike rider stopped and said, "You were really lucky, man."

"What you mean, 'lucky'?" the visitor grumbled. "That hurt!"

The cyclist replied, "Well, I usually drive a bus."

Have You Seen. . . ?

Uncle Ted bought a bike when he turned forty, and started riding ten miles a day. Now that he's forty-one, we have no idea where he is!

Riddle Roundup

When is a bicycle not a bicycle?
When it turns into a driveway.

Why can't an elephant ride a bicycle?
Because he doesn't have a thumb to ring the bell.

What is a ghost-proof bicycle?
One with no spooks.

EQUESTRIAN

That means "horse-related." And here's a great horse-related verse from the Bible: "Some trust in chariots and some in horses, but we trust in the name of the LORD our God" (Psalm 20:7). Now, with the serious stuff out of the way, let's laugh at some jokes!

....

Too Close

Nathan wanted to purchase a horse and went to a stable advertising one for sale. The seller, Joe, said, "This horse is definitely for you! But I do need to tell you that the man I got him from trained him, so there are some special instructions. He doesn't stop and go in the normal way. If you want him to stop, you need to use the command, "Down!" If you want him to go, you need to command him by saying, "Thank you!"

"Oh, that's no problem," Nathan said. "Can I take him out for a ride right now?"

"Sure," Joe replied.

Nathan got up into the saddle and the horse and rider took off through the field. Nathan was thrilled with the speed of the animal. But then he looked ahead and saw they were approaching a cliff at an alarming rate. Nathan tried to remember the command to stop. "Whoa!" he tried, but the horse kept racing along. "Stop!" he screamed, but the horse didn't stop. *What was the word?* They were just feet from the edge, when Nathan remembered. With fear in his voice, he yelled, "Down!"

The horse skidded to a stop with less than a foot left. Nathan was so relieved that he looked up, put his hands over his heart, and said, "Thank You!"

Medical Diagnosis

A horse jockey went to the doctor because he had severe stomach pain. After all the testing, the doctor found he had somehow ingested a plastic horse. They rushed him to surgery, where the plastic horse was removed from his stomach. The doctor now reports that his condition is stable.

Talkative Horse

A man was walking along a country road and saw a sign that said, TALKING HORSE FOR SALE. He was very skeptical but thought he would check it out and walked up the lane to the stable.

He saw a horse and approached it, feeling rather silly. But he had to try. "So, if you can talk, tell me what you've done during your lifetime."

"Well," the horse answered, "I was born in Kentucky and won the Derby two times. After I retired from racing, I was a member of the mounted police force and served in Dallas, Texas. A few years later, I was brought here, where I bring joy to children who want to come to the farm and ride a horse."

The man was stunned. He saw a farmer close by and asked, "Is this your horse?"

"Sure is," answered the farmer.

"Why in the world would you ever want to get rid of it? This is amazing! A talking horse!"

The farmer replied, "I'm just getting so tired of him makin' up stories. He never did any of that stuff he says!"

Sore Throat

A big race was coming up, and the jockey noticed his young horse coughing quite a bit. He called for the vet to come and check the horse out. The vet examined the pony, turned to the jockey, and said, "Son, there's absolutely nothing to worry about. He's just a little hoarse."

Bad Deal

It was a beautifully sunny day, and a man was out for a drive in the country. While passing a field, he noticed a stately horse standing under a tree. The man instantly had the idea that he would like to own that horse, so he stopped and asked the farmer who was working in the field if he could purchase the horse for one thousand dollars.

The farmer looked a bit surprised and replied, "I'm sorry. He isn't for sale. He doesn't look very good."

The man pressed on, saying, "He looks great to me! I'll give you twelve hundred dollars for him."

The farmer repeated himself and said, "I'm sorry. He isn't for sale. He doesn't look very good."

The man said, "Sir, if it's an issue of money, I'll increase my offer to fifteen hundred dollars. I'd really like that horse!"

The farmer thought for a moment and said, "Well, sonny, he doesn't look very good, but if you really want him that badly, you can have him."

The man paid the farmer and arranged to have him taken to his new home.

After one day with the horse, he went back to the farm and angrily shouted at the farmer, "You ripped me off! That horse is blind!"

"Well–I–I" drawled the farmer, "don't go gettin' mad at me. I told you he doesn't look very good, didn't I?"

Racing Horse

The owner of a racehorse took it to the vet for an exam after the animal faltered in a race. The man paced back and forth waiting for the vet's assessment. "So, doctor, will I ever be able to race him again?"

"Absolutely!" the vet answered. "And you'll probably beat him too!"

If Horses Could Talk. . .

"Don't you remember me?" the racehorse asked the other horse.

"Well–I–I," the horse answered slowly. "The pace is familiar, but I just cannot remember the mane."

Riddle Roundup

You are riding your horse when you realize there is an elephant in front of you and a tiger behind you. What do you do?
Get off the merry-go-round!

What is the best kind of story to tell a horse?
A tale of whoa.

How did the jockey ride to the race track on a Friday, stay for three days, and leave on a Friday?
His horse's name was Friday.

How can someone make a small fortune on horse racing?
Start with a large fortune.

Where do racehorses go to get their hair done?
Maine.

What is a racehorse's favorite bread?
Thoroughbred.

What do racehorses eat?
Fast food.

FISHING

Did you know that Jesus picked several fishermen to be part of His twelve disciples? If that isn't a thumbs-up for fishing, what is? We've caught a bunch of fishing jokes below. . .see if you think any of them are keepers.

....

A Fishy Story

Two avid fishermen go on a fishing vacation. They rent all the equipment: the reels, the rods, the waders, a rowboat, a car, even a cabin in the woods. They spend a bundle.

The first day they catch nothing. The same thing happens the second day and the third day. This continues until the last day of their vacation, when one of the men catches a fish.

While they're driving home, they're really depressed. One guy turns to the other and moans, "Do you realize that this one lousy fish we caught cost us fifteen hundred dollars?"

The other guy replies, "Wow! Good thing we didn't catch any more!"

Q & A

Q: What do fishermen and hypochondriacs have in common?

A: They don't really have to catch anything to be happy.

Q: Ten fishermen had a great day's catch at a small lake tucked away up country. Who was the saddest fish that evening?

A: The sole survivor.

A Glossary of Fishing Terms

catch and release: A conservation activity that usually happens when the local fish and game warden is within eyeshot of your boat.

line: Something you give your friends when they ask how your fishing went the past weekend.

reel: A rather heavy object that causes a rod to sink quickly when dropped overboard.

rod: A scientifically designed length of fiberglass that prevents a fisherman from getting too close to the fish.

school: A grouping in which fish are taught to avoid $29.99 lures and hold out for corn-flakes with peanut butter instead.

tackle: What your fishing partner did to you as you pulled in the catch of the day.

test: (1) The amount of strength a fishing line provides an angler when landing a fight-ing fish in a specific weight range; (2) A measure of your creativity in blaming "that stinkin' line" for once again losing the fish.

Lotsa Luck

Fishing season hadn't yet opened, and an angler was attempting to lure a trout when a stranger walked up. "Any luck?" he asked.

The fisherman boasted, "Any luck? Why, this is a wonderful spot. I took ten out of this stream yesterday."

"Is that so? By the way, do you know who I am?" the stranger asked.

"Nope."

"Well, meet the new game warden."

"Oh," gulped the fisherman. "Well, do you know who I am?"

"Nope."

"Meet the biggest liar in the county!"

Q & A

Q: What do you throw out when you need it
    and take in when you don't need it?

A: An anchor.

Smells Fishy

A fisherman accidentally left his day's catch under the seat of a bus. The next evening's newspaper had an ad that read, "If the person who left a bucket of fish on the number 52 bus would care to come to the garage, he can have the bus."

Ice Fishing

Max went ice fishing, but wasn't having much luck. He saw a guy across the way who was hauling in a bounty of fish. So Max went over and said, "What are you doing to catch all those fish? I'm just a few feet from you and I'm catching nothing."

The guy mumbled, "Ee yer erms orm."

Max didn't understand, and the fisherman tried again: "Ee yer erms orm."

Max looked confused, so the guy spit into his bait can. "*Spfff*. . .I said, 'keep your worms warm'!"

Calling All Witnesses

Al: I caught a twenty-pound salmon last week.
Sal: Were there any witnesses?
Al: There sure were. If there weren't, it would have been forty pounds.

Sit Still

Two serious fishermen were out in the middle of the lake. For almost two hours, neither of them moved a muscle. Then one became restless. "Jake," said his buddy, "that's the second time you've moved in twenty minutes. Did you come out here to fish or to dance?"

Bragging

A fisherman was bragging about a monster of a fish he caught. A friend broke in and said, "Yeah, I saw a picture of that fish, and he was all of a half pound."

"Yeah," said the proud fisherman. "But after battling for three hours, a fish can lose a lot of weight."

Earthworms, Huh?

Little Bubby and his dad were digging for bait in the garden. Bubby uncovered a centipede and held it up proudly.

"Oh Bub," his dad said, "that won't work. That's not an earthworm."

"Not an earthworm?" Bubby repeated. "What planet is it from?"

Environmental Fishing

The water in that stream is so polluted that if you catch a trout, he thanks you.

Fishy Intellect

The owner of a fish market was known for being intelligent and witty. All of his customers admired him and wondered what his secret was.

One man was shopping at the market one day and asked, "Kirk, what makes you so smart?"

Kirk lowered his voice and said, "Well, I wouldn't share my secret with just anybody, but since you're a great customer, I'll tell you. It's fish heads. If you eat enough of them, you will be absolutely brilliant."

"Fish heads?" asked the customer. "Do you sell those here?"

"Yes, I do," Kirk answered. "They're only three dollars each."

The customer bought five of them. One week later, he returned to the store. "Those fish heads are disgusting!" he exclaimed. "And besides, I don't feel any smarter."

"You must not have eaten enough then," said Kirk. So the customer bought ten fish heads and went home. Two weeks went by, and he returned to the store. He could barely contain his anger.

"Kirk," he began, "you've sold me twenty-five fish heads for three dollars each, but I can buy a whole fish for five dollars. You're ripping me off!"

"Well, see?" said Kirk. "It looks like you're getting smarter!"

Fighting Fishermen

What do you call two fishermen slapping each other with their boat's oars?
   Rowed rage.

Any Gators?

While a tourist was fishing off the Florida

coast, his boat capsized. Even though he could swim, he clung to the side of the up-turned boat because he was afraid of alligators. Spotting a beachcomber on the shore, he shouted out to him, "Are there any 'gators around here?"

"Nope," the man yelled back. "Ain't been any 'gators 'round these parts for years."

Feeling more at ease, the tourist commenced swimming leisurely toward shore. When he was about halfway there, he shouted out to the beachcomber again. "How'd you get rid of the 'gators?"

"Oh, we didn't do nothing," the beach-comber yelled back. "The sharks that came in ate every last one of them!"

You Serious?

A game warden came across a boy fishing near a No Fishing sign. "Didn't you see the sign, young man?" the warden asked.'

"Oh, I'm not fishing, sir," the boy answered. "Just teaching these worms to swim."

Heave-Ho!

Gary is a genuine, 100 percent, true sport fisherman. He once said that he caught a great white shark. Since it wasn't on display in his home, Freddie asked what happened to it. Gary sighed. "Well, it was too small to keep, so me and three other guys threw it back in."

A Bad Fit

Two old buddies went fishing, and one lost his dentures overboard. His friend, who was known to be a prankster, removed his own false teeth, tied them on his line, and pretended he had caught them.

Unhooking the teeth, his friend tried to put them into his mouth then threw them into the lake with disgust. "They're not mine!" he said. "They don't fit!"

Trick Fish

A man is walking from the lake carrying three fish in a bucket. He is approached by the game warden, who asks to see his fishing license.

The fisherman says to the warden, "I did not catch these fish; they are actually my pets. Every day I come down to the water and whistle, and these here fish jump out of the water into my bucket. I take them around to see the sights, and then I return them to the water at the end of the day."

"Oh, really?" The warden doesn't believe a word of the man's story and reminds him that it is against the law to fish without a valid license. The fisherman turns to the warden and says, "If you don't believe me, then just watch." He then throws all of the fish into the water.

The warden says, "Okay, now whistle to your fish and show me that they will jump out of the water and into your bucket."

"What fish?" asks the fisherman.

Little Kid

A boy sat on the side of a city street with his fishing line down a storm drain. Feeling sorry for him and wanting to humor him, a lady gave him fifty cents and kindly asked, "How many have you caught?"

"You're the tenth this morning," he replied.

Eye Problem

A man called in to work and told his boss, "I'm sorry. I won't make it in today."

When the boss asked why, the man replied, "I'm having a problem with my eyes."

"What's wrong with your eyes?" asked the boss.

"I just can't see coming to work," he said, "so I think I'll go fishing instead."

The Favorite

Two brothers, Mark and Matt, went fishing. Every time Mark threw his hook in, he caught a fish, but Matt didn't have the same success. By the end of the day, Mark had caught twelve fish, but Matt had caught nothing. The next day, Matt woke up very early in the morning, dressed in Mark's clothes, and carried Mark's rod. He went to the river and sat where Mark normally sat. He threw the hook in and waited.

Darkness cleared and the sun rose. After about two hours of waiting, a fish popped out of the water and asked Matt, "Where is Mark?"

Meditation

Old fishermen never die; they just smell that way.

Ice Fishing

Paisley wanted to go ice fishing. She had read several books on the subject, and finally, after purchasing all of the equipment she would need, she carefully made her way over the ice.

She found what she thought was a good spot and set up her stool. She took out a tool and started to make a circular cut in the ice.

After about thirty seconds, she heard a voice from above that boomed, "There are no fish under the ice." It startled Paisley, and she dropped her tool. But she figured she must be hearing things, so she steadied herself and once again began cutting the hole.

Once again, a voice bellowed, "There are no fish under the ice." She looked around and couldn't see anyone, and she wondered if someone was pulling a prank. She confidently picked up her tool and continued cutting the hole.

Again, a voice called out, "There are no fish under the ice." Paisley stopped, closed her eyes, and asked, "Is that You, Lord?"

"No," answered the voice. "This is the manager of the skating rink."

Riddle Roundup

What is the difference between a fisherman
and a lazy student?
> *One baits his hook; the other hates his book.*

What is a fish's favorite game?
> *Salmon says.*

What Spanish musical instrument helps you
fish?
> *A cast-a-net.*

What do atomic scientists do when they go
on vacation?
> *They go fission.*

What is the best way to communicate with a
fish?
> *Drop him a line.*

How do you keep a fish from smelling?
> *Plug its nose.*

Why don't fish like to play tennis?
> *Because they're afraid of the net.*

What do fish take to stay healthy?
> *Vitamin sea.*

What do you call fish with no eyes?
> *Fsh.*

Why is it so easy to weigh fish?
  Because they always come with scales.

What do fish use when they want to buy something?
  Sand dollars.

Where does a fish deposit his money?
  In the river bank.

What is the difference between a piano and a fish?
  You can tune a piano but you can't tuna fish.

Why do fish swim in schools?
  Because they can't walk.

What kind of music should you play when fishing?
  Something catchy!

FOOTBALL

Today, "Saints versus Lions" is an NFL
game between New Orleans and Detroit.
Back in the Old Testament, it might have
described Daniel's night in the den of
the big cats. (P.S. Daniel won!)

....

Makes You Go "Hmmm. . ."

Football is a game where twenty-two big,
strong players run around like crazy while
eighty thousand people who really need the
exercise sit in the stands and watch them.

Now That's Loyalty

Tim was an avid Kansas City Chiefs fan, but
he had a really lousy seat location. Squinting
through his binoculars, he spotted an empty
seat on the fifty-yard line and rushed down to
try to snag it.

When he got there, Tim asked the man
sitting next to it, "Is this seat taken?" The man
replied, "This was my wife's seat. Like me, she
was a big fan, but she passed away."

Tim replied, "I'm so sorry to hear of your
loss. May I ask why you didn't give her ticket

to a friend or relative?"

The man replied, "They're all at the funeral."

A Football Riddle

Which insect makes the worst quarterback?
The fumble-bee.

College Entrance Exam for Football Players

(Time limit: three weeks)

What language is spoken in France?

_____

Give the first name of Thomas Jefferson.

_____

Would you ask William Shakespeare to:
Build a bridge _____
Sail the ocean _____
Lead an army _____
WRITE A PLAY _____

What time is it when the big hand is on the twelve and the little hand is on the five?

_____

Metric conversion: How many feet is 0.0 meters? _____

How many commandments was Moses given? (approximately) _____

What are people in America's far north called?

Westerners _____
Southerners _____
Northerners _____

Spell:

Bush _____
Airplane _____
Dog _____

Six kings of England have been named George, the last being George the Sixth. Name the previous five. _____

Where does rain come from?

Cars _____
A store _____
Canada _____
The sky _____

What are coat hangers for? _____

Advanced math: If you have three apples, how many do you have? _____

What does NBC (National Broadcasting Corp.) stand for? _____

You must answer three or more questions correctly to qualify.

Missing Football

A man holding a football leaned over his garden gate and shouted to two boys on the other side of the street, "Is this your ball?" "Did it do any damage, mister?" one boy asked.

"No, it didn't."

"Then it's ours."

Sister, Sister

Two elderly sisters donated five dollars to a charity and, to their surprise, won tickets to a football game. Since they had never seen a live football game, Madge thought the free tickets would provide some fun for her and her sister.

"I think so too," said Mabel. "Let's go!"

They soon found themselves high in a noisy stadium overlooking a large grassy expanse. They watched the kickoff and the seemingly endless back and forth struggles throughout the scoreless first half.

They enjoyed the band music and cheer-leader performance that followed.

Then came the second half. When the teams lined up for the second half kickoff, Madge nudged her sister. "I guess we can go home now, Mabel," she said. "This is where we came in."

Another Football Riddle

Why was the pig thrown out of the football game?

The refs said he was playing dirty.

Huddle Talk

One NFL team has had so many members in trouble with the law, they've adopted a new "Honor System": "Yes, your Honor. No, your Honor."

Good Question!

The football team was playing terribly. In desperation, the coach ran over to a player on the bench and said, "I want you to go out there and get mean and tough!"

"Okay, Coach," said the player. He jumped to his feet and asked, "Which one's Mean, and which one's Tough?"

What's in a Name?

The coach asked his assistant, "What's that new fullback's name?"

The assistant said, "He's from Thailand. His name is Bandanakadriy-ariki."

The coach said, "I hope he's good. That'll get me even with the reporters."

Tough Call

It was a particularly tough football game, and nerves were on edge. The home team had been the victims of three or four close calls, and they were now trailing the visitors by a touchdown and a field goal. When the official called yet another close one in the visitors' favor, the home quarterback blew his top.

"How many times can you do this in a

single game?" he screamed. "You were wrong on the out-of-bounds. You were wrong on that last first down, and you missed an illegal tackle in the first quarter."

The official just stared.

The quarterback seethed, but he suppressed the language that might get him tossed from the game. "What it comes down to," he bellowed, "is that you stink!"

The official stared a few more seconds. Then he bent down, picked up the ball, paced off fifteen yards, and put the ball down. He turned to face the steaming quarterback. "And how do I smell from over here?" he calmly asked.

Water Boy

There was a football player who was a bit deficient academically. Finally, the dean told the young man he could play in the big game if he would memorize the formula for water: H_2O.

The morning of the big day, the dean called the young player into his office and asked him to recite the formula for water. The player grinned and recited, "H I J K L M N O."

Crowd Pleaser

Troy: Back in the old days, I played in front of thousands of people at the college stadium.
Payton: Really? You played football?
Troy: No, drums in the band.

Fast Ones

One of our linebackers is so huge he should have a license plate instead of a number.

Did you hear about the center who wasn't that bright? They had to stencil on his pants, THIS END UP. On his shoes they put T.G.I.F.: TOES GO IN FIRST.

A formerly hopeful football player: "I gave up my hope of being a star halfback the second day of practice. One tackle grabbed my left leg, another grabbed my right, and the linebacker looked at me and said, 'Make a wish!'"

The placekicker missed his attempt at a field goal. He was so angry, he went to kick himself. . .and missed again.

First Timer

Ben took his little brother to his first football game. Afterward, he asked him how he liked the game.

"I liked it, but I couldn't understand why they were killing each other for twenty-five cents," he replied.

"What do you mean?"

"Well, everyone kept yelling, 'Get the quarterback!' "

The Truth Hurts

What do you call a Cleveland Brown at the Super Bowl?

A spectator.

Locker Talker

A well-known college football coach admitted, "I give the same halftime speech over and over. It works best when my players are better than the other coach's players."

Football is not a contact sport. It's a collision sport. Dancing is a good example of a contact sport.

Q & A

Q: How many college football players does it take to change a light bulb?

A: The entire team! And they all get a semester's credit for it.

Q: If you live in Green Bay, Wisconsin, how do you keep bears out of your backyard?

A: Put up goalposts.

More Fast Ones

Our players have a lot on the ball. Unfortunately, it's never their hands.

Some chickens were in the yard when a football flew over the fence. A rooster walked by and said, "I'm not complaining, girls, but look at the work they're doing next door!"

I would have played football, but I have an intestinal problem—no guts.

Coach Smith retired due to illness and fatigue. The fans were sick and tired of him.

We have so many players on the disabled list the team bus can park in a handicapped space.

The only way they can gain yardage is to run their game films backwards.

Blame Game

Three fans were complaining about how bad their local pro team was. The first fan blamed the team owner: "If he wasn't so cheap, he could sign better players. We'd have a great team." The second fan blamed the players themselves: "If they worked harder, we'd win more games." The third fan blamed his own parents: "If I'd been born in a different city, I could support a decent team!"

Turkey Ball

The pro football team had just finished its daily practice when a large turkey came strutting onto the field. While the players gazed in amazement, the turkey walked up to the head coach and demanded a tryout. Everyone stared in silence as the turkey caught pass after pass and ran through the defensive line.

When the turkey returned to the sidelines, the coach shouted, "You're terrific! Sign up for the season, and I'll see to it that you get a huge signing bonus."

"Forget the bonus," the turkey said. "All I want to know is, does the season go past Thanksgiving Day?"

What's a Fan?

A football fan is a guy who'll yell at the quarterback for not spotting an open receiver forty-five yards away, then head for the parking lot and not be able to find his own car.

Knock, Knock

Knock, knock.
Who's there?
Wilbur Wright.
Wilbur Wright who?
Wilbur Wright back for the second half, after these messages.

Sports Laws

Whoever thought up "It's only a game" probably just lost one.

It is always unlucky to be behind at the end of the game.

The trouble with being a good sport is that you have to lose to prove it.

Another Chance

A football coach walked into the locker room before the game, looked at his star player and said, "I'm not supposed to let you play since you failed math, but we need you in there. So what I have to do is ask you a math question, and if you get it right, you can play."

The player agreed, so the coach looked into his eyes intently and said, "Now concentrate hard and tell me the answer to this. What is two plus two?"

The player thought for a moment and then answered, "Four."

"Did you say four?" the coach asked, excited that he got it right.

Suddenly all the other players began yelling, "Come on, Coach, give him another chance!"

Animal Super Bowl

During a recent Super Bowl, there was another football game of note between big animals and small animals. The big animals were crushing the small animals. At half-time, the coach made an impassioned speech to rally the little animals.

At the start of the second half, the big

animals had the ball. On the first play, an elephant got stopped for no gain. On the second play, the rhino was stopped for no gain. On the third down, the hippo was thrown for a five-yard loss.

The defense huddled around the coach, who asked excitedly, "Who stopped the elephant?"

"I did," said the centipede.

"Who stopped the rhino?"

"Uh, that was me too," said the centipede.

"And how about the hippo? Who hit him for a five-yard loss?"

"Well, that was me as well," said the centipede.

"So where were you during the first half?" demanded the coach.

"Well," said the centipede, "I was having my ankles taped."

Riddle Roundup

Why is an airline pilot like a football player?
 They both want to make safe touchdowns.

What kind of tea do football players drink?
 Penal-tea.

What is a cheerleader's favorite color?
 Yeller.

What did the football say to the football player?

"I get a kick out of you."

Why did the football team take string to the game?

So they could tie the score.

Which football player wears the biggest helmet?

The one with the biggest head.

What is the difference between a football player and a dog?

A football player has a complete uniform, but the dog only pants.

What did the football coach say to the broken vending machine?

"Give me my quarterback!"

GOLF

Golf is a game in which the *lowest* score wins. That can be confusing, kind of like Jesus' saying, "the last will be first, and the first last" (Matthew 20:16). Let that one rattle around in your brain while you read the following golf jokes:

....

Caddy Trouble

Golfer: Notice any improvement since I saw you last year?

Caddy: Hmm. . .you polished your clubs, didn't you?

Golfer: Why do you keep looking at your watch?

Caddy: This isn't a watch, sir. It's a compass.

Golfer: Caddy, why didn't you see where that ball went?

Caddy: Well, it doesn't usually go anywhere when you swing. You caught me off guard.

The Foursome

Four old men were playing a round of golf. "These hills are getting steeper as the years go by," one complained.

"The sand traps seem to be bigger than I remember them too," said another senior.

After hearing enough, the oldest and wisest of the four, at eighty-seven, said, "Just be thankful we're still on the right side of the grass!"

Widely Known

One day, Justin Brown went to play a round of golf at a different course, just to see if he could do better somewhere other than where he normally played. He hired a caddy to guide him around the course. After another day of slices, bad putts, and duff shots, he was visibly upset. He turned to the caddy and said glumly, "You know, I must be the worst golfer in the world."

"Oh no, sir," the caddy said, attempting to encourage him. "I've heard there is a guy across town named Justin Brown—he's the worst player in the world!"

Newbie

When Mr. McKenna retired, his coworkers gave him a goodbye gift, a set of golf clubs. After looking at them for a few weeks, he finally decided he'd try the game. He asked the local pro for lessons, explaining that he knew nothing about the game.

The pro showed him the stance and swing, then said, "Just hit the ball toward the flag on the first green."

Novice McKenna teed up and smacked the ball straight down the fairway and onto the green, where it stopped inches from the hole.

"Now what?" McKenna asked the speechless pro.

"Uh, you're supposed to hit the ball into the cup," the pro finally said, after regaining his composure.

"Oh, great! Now you tell me," said the beginner disgustedly.

Great Score

George came home from a game of golf, and his neighbor asked how he did. "Oh, I shot seventy," said George.

"That's a great score!" replied the neighbor.

"Yeah," George said. "Tomorrow I'll play the second hole."

Weekend Game

Two men are talking at work on a Monday morning.

"What did you do over the weekend?"

"Dropped hooks into water."

"Oh, went fishing, huh?"

"No, golfing."

Quit Playing When. . .

- You can remember for a week the one good shot you had in the round.
- The ball retriever is the most used piece of equipment in your bag.
- You and your group have rules for mulligans.
- The club has named a pond in front of the green after you.

No Kiddin'?

Harry: You know what your main golf problem is?

Terry: What?

Harry: You stand too close to the ball after you've hit it.

Silent Treatment

Many golfers prefer a golf cart to a caddy because the cart cannot count, criticize, or laugh.

Safe secret

A businessman frequently left the office to play golf and instructed his secretary to tell anyone who called only that he was away from his desk. After he left the office one day, a friend he was planning to meet called the office. He had forgotten which course they had decided to play.

When the secretary answered, he asked for her boss, but she would only say that he was away from his desk.

"Please tell me," said the exasperated golfer, "exactly how far away from his desk is he? Is he five miles away at the country club or seven miles away at Clearview?"

Yuck, Yuck

Q: Why do golfers wear two pairs of pants?
A: In case they get a hole in one.

Golf Business

Jason, looking depressed, says to his friend, "My doctor tells me I can't play golf."

"So he's played with you too, huh?"

Heavenly Golf

Toward the end of a particularly trying round of golf, Troy was the picture of frustration. He'd hit too many rotten shots. Finally he blurted to his caddie, "I'd move heaven and earth to break a hundred on this course."

"Try heaven," replied the caddie. "You've already moved most of the earth."

Record Breaker

Brian and Randy were talking about their golf games. Brian said, "I got kicked off the course today for breaking sixty."

Randy looked at him in amazement. "Breaking sixty?" he said. "That's incredible!"

Brian smiled and replied, "Yeah, I never knew a golf cart could go that fast!"

Golf Ball

Dave and Tim both liked to golf. One day, Dave went to Tim and said, "Hey, look at this great ball!"

"What's so great about it?" asked Tim.

"Well," Dave said, "if you lose it, it will beep until you find it, and if it goes into the water, it will float. This ball is impossible to lose."

"Wow!" exclaimed Tim. "Where in the world did you get that?"

"Oh," answered Dave. "I found it."

Temper, Temper

A golfer was playing a round with his buddies. On the seventh hole, he had to hit the ball over a pond. He became so frustrated after hitting the fifth ball into the pond that he picked up his golf bag and heaved it into the water, then strode off the course.

Suddenly, he turned around, jumped into the lake, and dove under the water. His buddies, stunned at the events, thought he was changing his mind and attempting to salvage his clubs. But when he exited the water, he didn't have the bag or the clubs.

As the wet golfer walked away, one of

his buddies asked, "Why did you jump into the pond?"

"Because," the man muttered, "I left my keys in the bag."

Mathematical Golfer

One day a math teacher and his brother were out golfing. The brother was to tee off first, and just after he swung, he yelled, "Fore!"

The math teacher was up next. Just after he swung, he yelled, "Square root of sixty-four divided by two!"

Course Mishap

A wife began to get a little worried after her husband had been out golfing for the day and hadn't returned by dusk. Around 7:00, the husband called his wife. "Where have you been?" she asked. "You should have been home hours ago!"

"Well, John broke his ankle on the fourth hole."

"That's terrible!" exclaimed the wife.

"I know," agreed her husband. "All day long it was hit the ball, carry John; hit the ball, carry John. . . ."

Out Golfing

Bubba and Goober were out golfing. They were stuck on the sixteenth green when a foursome arrived to play through. One guy asked, "What seems to be the trouble?"

Bubba answered, "We both hit to the green and when we got here, one ball was in the cup and one was balanced on the edge of the cup. We can't figure out who got the hole in one."

The golfer looked at the two balls and replied, "Which one of you was playing with the orange ball?"

Well, Sonny. . .

Young Alfie was an avid golfer, so one afternoon when he found himself with a few hours to spare, he decided to get in nine holes before he had to head home.

Just as Alfie was about to tee off, an old gentleman walked onto the tee and asked if he could play along with him for a twosome. "I suppose so," Alfie responded.

To his surprise, the old man played fairly quickly. He didn't hit the ball too far, but he plodded along consistently and didn't waste any time.

Finally, they reached the ninth fairway, and Alfie found himself with a tough shot. There was a large pine tree right in front of his ball and directly between his ball and the green.

After several minutes of watching Alfie debate how to hit the shot, the old man finally said, "You know, when I was your age, I'd hit the ball right over that tree."

With that challenge before him, Alfie swung hard and hit the ball right smack into the top of the tree. It dropped back to the ground not a foot from where it originally lay.

"Of course," the old man commented, "when I was your age, that pine tree was only six feet tall."

About Golfers. . .

There are thousands of people who are worse golfers than he is. Of course, they don't play.

I'm not saying his game is bad, but if he grew tomatoes, they'd come up sliced.

One of the quickest ways to meet new people is to pick up the wrong ball.

He cut ten strokes off his score. He stopped playing the last hole.

Fishing for a Compliment

Eddie: What do you think of my game?
Caddie: It's okay, but I like golf better.

Golf pro: Are you two ladies here to learn to
    play golf?
First lady: My friend is. I learned yesterday.

Wife: You're so involved with golf that you
    can't remember the day we were married.
Husband: That's what you think. It was the
    same day I sank a thirty-five-foot putt.

Anonymous Confession

"I don't play golf. Personally, I think there's
something wrong with any game in which the
person who gets to hit the ball the most is
the loser."

Coincidence

"You must be the worst caddie in the world,"
said the dejected golfer after a disastrous
afternoon on the course.

    "I doubt it, sir," replied the caddie. "That
would be too much of a coincidence."

A Substitution

Official: Too bad, sir, we have no open time on the course today.

Golfer: Hey, just a minute—what if Tiger Woods showed up? I bet you'd have a starting time for him. Right?

Official: Of course.

Golfer: Well, I happen to know he won't be here today, so we'll take his tee time.

Short Putts

She: Let me get this straight. The less I hit the ball, the better I am doing.

He: That's right.

She: Then why hit it at all?

Honest Assessment

As the golfer said, "I know I can play better than this. I just never have."

More Short Putts

In golf, you drive for show and putt for dough.

Golf is a game where the ball lies poorly and the players well.

Real golfers don't cry when they line up their fourth putt.

Golf is an easy game—it's just hard to play.

Questions Better Left Unasked

Kim said to her friend, "I just don't understand why Mike likes to golf so much."

"I know," responded Rachel. "I went golfing with Roger once, and he told me I asked way too many questions."

"Well, I'm sure you were just trying to understand the game," said Kim. "What did you ask?"

"Oh, just things like, 'Why did you hit that ball into the lake?' "

Bah!

The club grouch was unhappy about everything: the food, the fees, the parking, the other members. The first time he hit a hole-in-one he complained, "And I could really have used the putting practice!"

What Golf Is

Bob Hope once said, "If you watch a game, it's fun. If you play it, it's recreation. If you work at it, it's golf."

Perspective

A golfer is teeing up on a course overlooking a river. He calls his partner's attention to a couple of fishermen in a boat. "Look at those two dummies, fishing in the rain!"

Senior Golfing

Benjamin was eighty years old and could hit a great round of golf, but his eyesight was failing, and he couldn't see where the ball landed. He asked ninety-two-year-old Ed to go with him. Ed could no longer hit the ball, but his eyes were perfect. Benjamin teed off and turned to Ed and asked, "Did you see where the ball landed?"

Ed replied, "Sure did."

"Well," said Benjamin, "where is it?"

"I forget," said Ed.

Riddle Roundup

What did the dentist say to the golfer?
"You have a hole in one."

Where do golfers dance?
At the golf ball.

What is a golfer's favorite letter?
Tee.

GYMNASTICS

When airplanes were first invented, some people said, "If God wanted humans to fly, He would have given them wings." Wonder what they'd say about modern gymnasts who jump so high and twirl through the air?

....

New Student

A mom wanted to sign her daughter up for gymnastics classes. She decided she would make a phone call to get more information. The desk attendant at the gym answered the phone and listened as the mom explained that she was interested in classes for her five-year-old daughter. "Can she do splits?" asked the attendant.

"No, she can't," answered the mom.

"How flexible is she?" asked the worker.

"Well, she really can't do Tuesdays or Fridays."

Tumbler

Sometimes I tuck my knees into my chest and then tip forward. That's just how I roll.

Fictional Gymnastics Book Titles

Uneven Bars by Jim Nastiks
Floor Routines by Flip Over

Riddle Roundup

How long does it take for a gymnast to get to practice?

A split second.

What do you get if you cross a fruit and a gymnast?

An apple turnover.

What do a credit card and a gymnast have in common?

They both have outstanding balance.

What do gymnasts like on their popcorn?

Somersalt.

Did you hear about the gymnast who once had a fear of vaulting?

He finally got over it.

HIKING/CAMPING/ THE GREAT OUTDOORS

The great outdoors are great because God made them that way, full of mountains, rivers, lakes, trees, fields. . .and bears. Let's just hope those bears aren't hungry!

....

Missing Milky Way

Sherlock Holmes and Dr. Watson were on a camping trip. The first night out they had gone to bed and were lying looking up at the sky. "Watson," the great detective said, "look up. What do you see?"

"Well, I see thousands of stars."

"And what does that mean to you?"

"Well, I guess it means we will have another nice day tomorrow. What does that mean to you, Holmes?"

"To me, it means someone has stolen our tent."

Tent Woes

Park Ranger: What's wrong, son?

Camper: I have a camouflage tent.

Park Ranger: What's wrong with that?

Camper: I've looked everywhere, and I just can't find it.

Over the River

One day three men were hiking along and came upon a wide, raging river. They needed to get to the other side, but it looked impossible to cross, and they had no idea how to do it.

Suddenly, they spotted what looked to be a magic lamp on the bank of the river. One of the men picked it up, rubbed it, and out came a genie. "I will grant you each one wish," said the genie.

The first man said, "I would like to have the strength to cross this river."

Poof! The man instantly had big, strong arms and legs and was able to swim across the river—though it took him almost two hours to do it.

Seeing this, the second man said, "I wish to have the strength and ability to cross this river."

Poof! A rowboat appeared, and the second man was able to row across the river—though it took him almost an hour to do it.

The third man had seen how well things had gone for his two buddies, so he made his wish, saying, "I wish for the strength, ability and intelligence to cross this river."

Poof! In his hands he found a trail map, and within a minute, he walked across the bridge.

Another Bear

Two backpackers saw a bear about to charge them. One of the hikers took off his boots and put on running shoes. His friend said, "You'll never outrun the bear—why are you putting those shoes on?"

The guy with the running shoes responded, "I don't have to outrun the bear. I just have to outrun you."

Practical Camping Hints

When using a public campground, a tuba placed on your picnic table will keep the sites on either side of you vacant.

You can duplicate the warmth of a down-filled sleeping bag by climbing into a plastic garbage bag with several geese.

When camping, always wear a long-sleeved shirt. It gives you something to wipe your nose on.

A hot rock placed in your sleeping bag will keep your feet warm. A hot enchilada works almost as well, but the cheese sticks between your toes.

Lost Hiker

Exhausted hiker: I am so glad to see you!
 I've been lost for three days!
Other hiker: Well, don't get too excited.
 I've been lost for a week.

The Other Side

A lost hiker is on one side of a raging river and sees another hiker on the other side. There are no bridges, and he has no boat. "Hey there!" he shouted to the hiker on the opposite side. "How do I get to the other side?"

The other hiker responded with, "You *are* on the other side!"

Tips for Campers

Get even with the bear who raided your food container by kicking his favorite stump apart and eating all the ants.

A two-man pup tent does not include two men or a pup.

A potato baked in the coals for one hour makes an excellent side dish. A potato baked in the coals for three hours makes an excellent hockey puck.

Always Prepared

Sam was in Cub Scouts, and couldn't wait until the school year ended so he could get into the outdoors. His teacher, Mr. Brown, knew how much Sam loved camping, and used that as an example in a math question.

"So, Sam, if I gave you two tents, then another two tents, and then another two tents, how many tents would you have?"

Sam quickly answered, "Seven."

"No," Mr. Brown replied. "Listen carefully, Sam. If I gave you two tents, then another two tents, and then another two tents, how many tents would you have?"

"Seven," Sam said again.

Mr. Brown sighed. "Let's try this another way. If I gave you two apples, then another two apples, and then another two apples, how many would you have?"

"Six," Sam replied.

"Good!" Mr. Brown said. "So if I gave you two tents, and then another two tents, and then another two tents, how many tents would you have?"

Sam was frustrated. "Seven!"

Mr. Brown was frustrated too. "Sam, why do you keep answering 'seven'?"

"Because I already *own* a tent!"

Riddle Roundup

What is the first thing you put on a trail?
Your feet.

What wears shoes but has no feet?
The sidewalk.

Why do you always start a hike with the right foot first?
Because when you move one foot, the other one is always left.

What has a foot on each side and one in the middle?

　　A yardstick.

HOCKEY

A good verse for hockey players: "If it is possible, as far as it depends on you, live at peace with everyone" (Romans 12:18).

....

Smile!

A dentist was recently heard complimenting a goalie on his nice, even teeth: one, three, five, seven, nine, and eleven were missing.

More Teeth

Hockey players have been complaining about violence for years. It's just that without their teeth, no one can understand them.

They say there are three ways to play hockey: rough, rougher, and "I'll help you find your teeth if you'll help me look for mine."

Good Point

Why do hockey players spend all their time on ice?
Because their skates would bog down in the sand.

Hockey Ponderings

I think hockey is a great game. Of course, I have a dad who's a dentist.

I knew it was going to be a wild game when a fight broke out in the middle of the National Anthem.

Injurious Hockey

Andy came to work limping like crazy. One of his coworkers noticed and asked Andy what happened.

"Oh, nothing," Andy replied. "It's just an old hockey injury that acts up once in a while."

"Gee, I never knew you played hockey," the coworker responded.

"No, I don't," explained Andy. "I hurt it last year when my favorite player was sent to the penalty box. I put my foot through the television screen."

You May Be a Hockey Nut If. . .

You think there are three periods in basketball.

Bumper Sticker

Be Kind to Animals. Hug a Hockey Player.

Q & A

Q: What is a hockey puck?
A: It's a hard rubber disc that players hit when they are not hitting each other.

Q: What's the difference between a hockey game and a prize fight?
A: In a hockey game, the fights are real.

Advantages of Being a Goalie

- Padding gives the impression that you're really buff.
- Helmet allows you to double as Darth Vader in any upcoming *Star Wars* movie.
- Bruises can really bring out the color of your eyes.

Riddle Roundup

How does a hockey player kiss?
  He puckers up.

What do you give a hockey player when he demands money?

A check.

HUNTING

Ever hear of Nimrod? According to the Bible, he was "a mighty hunter before the LORD" (Genesis 10:9). To hear them tell it today, there are a lot of Nimrods out tramping through the woods!

....

Duck Hunters

Phil and Gil were duck hunting. For five hours, they had been unable to bag anything. Finally, one turned to the other and suggested "Maybe we ought to try throwing the dogs a little bit higher."

An Unbearable Situation

Bill was telling his buddy what a great hunter he was. When they arrived at their cabin, Bill suggested, "You get the fire started, and I'll go shoot us something for supper."

In a few minutes, Bill met a grizzly bear. He dropped his gun and took off for the cabin, with the bear in hot pursuit. When he was a few feet away from the cabin, Bill tripped over a log. The bear couldn't stop and skidded through the open cabin door.

Bill got up, slammed the door, and yelled to his friend inside, "You skin that one, and I'll go get us another one."

Mistaken Identity

Guide: I don't guide hunters anymore, only fishermen.
Hunter: Why?
Guide: I have never been mistaken for a fish.

Which Way?

One hunter to another: "Look at those bear tracks! I'll go see where he came from, and you can go see where he went."

End of the Season

The Wednesday night church service happened to fall on the last day of hunting season. When the pastor asked his congregation if anyone had bagged a deer this year, not a hand was raised.

Puzzled, the pastor said, "I don't understand. Many of you wives said your husbands were missing last Sunday because of hunting. So to help in your hunting quest, I asked the congregation to pray for your deer and safety."

"It sure worked," groaned one hunter. "They deer are *all* safe."

Dead Duck

Three men went duck hunting one day. Two of them heard many stories from the third about his "great" duck hunting prowess. After a few hours, each of the first two men had bagged a couple of ducks, but their bragging friend hadn't taken a shot. They questioned him, so he agreed to show his shooting abilities at the next opportunity.

A few moments later, one lone duck flew by. As promised, the boaster stood up and squeezed out one shot. The duck kept flying.

"Gentlemen, you have just witnessed a miracle," he said, "because there flies a dead duck!"

The Pessimist

An avid duck hunter was on the lookout for a new bird dog. His search ended when he found a dog that could walk on water to retrieve a duck. Shocked by his find, he was sure none of his friends would believe it.

The first time he took the dog out, he was joined by a very pessimistic friend. As they waited by the lakeshore, a flock of ducks flew by. They fired, and a duck fell into the lake. The dog responded like a flash. Sure as anything, it walked across the water to retrieve the bird, never getting more than his paws wet.

The pessimistic friend saw everything but didn't say a word.

On the drive home, the dog's owner asked, "Did you notice anything unusual about my new dog?"

"I sure did," responded his friend. "He can't swim."

Planning Ahead

A father took his boy tiger hunting. They were creeping through the underbrush when the dad said, "Son, this hunt marks your passage into manhood. Do you have any questions?"

"Yes, Dad. If the tiger attacks you, how do I get home?"

Tracking

Three hunters were stranded in the mountains, and they didn't think they'd be able to get back to civilization for three days. So they all made a plan that each night one would get the food.

The first night, the first guy went out and came back with a big deer, causing the man who was to go out the next night to hunt for food to ask for advice. The successful first hunter admitted to the next hunter that he scored by finding tracks, following tracks, and then shooting the deer.

The next night, the second hunter went out and scored.

The third night, the third hunter went out to get a deer and came back hours later, all shaken up. The other two hunters asked, "What happened?" The shaken guy said he went out, found some tracks, followed them . . .and barely missed getting hit by a train.

Wild Shots

When he was fined for using last year's hunting license, Zeke claimed, "I was only shooting at the ones I missed last year."

License or No License

A hunter just tagged his deer as the game warden walked up. "Where's your license?" asked the warden.

"Don't know," replied the hunter.

"Okay, you're under arrest for no license. Follow me to the road, and help me drag the deer," returned the warden.

"No way," answered the hunter. "You drag it."

Two hours later, after the warden had dragged the deer to the road, the hunter remembered which pocket held his license.

Prayer of Blessing

A pastor skipped service one Sunday to go bear hunting in the mountains. As he turned a corner along the path, he and a bear collided. The pastor stumbled backwards, slipped off the trail, and began tumbling down the mountain with the bear in hot pursuit. Finally, the pastor crashed into a boulder, breaking both of his legs and sending his rifle flying. Lying there, unable to move or defend himself with the bear coming closer, the pastor cried out in desperation, "Lord, I repent for all I've done. Forgive me for not being in church. Please make this bear a Christian!"

The bear skidded to a halt at the pastor's feet, falling to his knees and clasping his paws together. "Lord," he said, "I do thank You for the food I am about to receive."

Hunting Brain-Teaser

Two fathers and two sons went duck hunting. Each shot a duck, but they shot only three ducks in all. How come?

The hunters were a man, his son, and his grandson.

Riddle Roundup

How do you catch a unique deer?
Younique up on it.

How do you catch a tame deer?
Tame way. . .younique up on it.

Which side of a deer has the most meat?
The inside.

MARCHING BAND

Did you know that a marching band conquered the powerful Bible city called Jericho? "On the seventh day, they got up at daybreak and marched around the city seven times. . . . The seventh time around, when the priests sounded the trumpet blast, Joshua commanded the army, 'Shout! For the LORD has given you the city!' . . . At the sound of the trumpet, when the men gave a loud shout, the wall collapsed; so everyone charged straight in, and they took the city" (Joshua 6:15–16, 20). That's one tough band.

....

What Time Is It?

Fran: "What time is it?"

Jan: "I don't know. Hand me that trombone and I'll find out."

   (Blows trombone loudly.)

Voice yelling from outside: *"Who is playing the trombone at 5:00 a.m.?!"*

Ultimatum

Athletic director: How did you get the band's
    lines so straight for the halftime show?
Band leader: Land mines.

Riddle Roundup

Why are drums so cool?
    They're hard to beat!

What's the difference between a flute and
a tuna?
    *You can tune a flute, but you can't flute
a tuna!*

How do you make a bandstand?
    Take away their chairs.

What do you call a documentary about the
history of the trombone?
    A slide show.

What was the cat playing in the marching
band?
    Purr-cussion.

What do talented trumpet players have in
common with pirates?
    They can both hit the high C's.

Why did the marching band director recruit a trumpet-playing cow?

He was a great moo-sician.

In what month do bands parade the most?

March.

What do color guard and penalized football players have in common?

They get flagged.

If the tubas stand behind the trumpets, what comes after the tubas?

The three-bas.

Which marching band member can jump higher than the judges' table?

All of them. A table can't jump.

How do you fix a broken tuba?

With a tuba glue!

How many saxophones were in the marching band?

Tenor so.

MARTIAL ARTS

Wouldn't you just like to do
a karate chop on the devil?

....

Martial Arts Quip

My friend went into martial arts just for the
kick of it.

Riddle Roundup

What do you call a pig that knows martial
arts?
    Pork chop.

What kind of martial arts does a gorilla
excel in?
    Kong Fu.

What kind of martial arts are soybeans
trained in?
    Tofu.

How did the karate instructor greet his class?
    He said, "Hi-yah!"

OLYMPICS

Seriously—there were Olympic games going on when Jesus lived on earth. But we don't believe there were any cereal boxes with the athletes' faces on them. . . .

....

Ladies and Gentlemen

The leader of the Olympics host country opened the Olympic Games by reading his speech.

"Oh," he said. "Oh, oh, oh, oh."

An aide nudged him. "Uh, sir," he said, "you're reading the Olympic symbol."

Fictional Olympics Book Titles

Racing Downhill by Bob Sled
Winning Gold by Vic Tory
Champions by Ima Winner
Reaching the Finish Line by Ray Sur

Riddle Roundup

Why couldn't the Olympian listen to music?
Because he broke the record.

Why did the fastest cat get disqualified from the Olympics?

It was a cheetah.

What did the hot dog say when it earned a gold medal?

"I'm a wiener!"

What is the best part of an Olympics boxer's jokes?

The punch line.

POOL (BILLIARDS)

No, the Pool of Siloam (John 9:7) was not a place to play billiards. But we hope you have a ball with these pool jokes.

....

Unhealthy Eating Habits

"My stomach has been bothering me, doctor" the patient complained.

"Tell me what you have been eating," said the doctor.

"I only eat pool balls," the patient confessed.

"Pool balls?" the astonished doctor repeated. "That has to be the problem. What kind do you eat?"

"All kinds," answered the patient. "Yellow and black ones for breakfast, red and orange ones at lunch, white ones for snacks, and blue and purple ones for dinner."

"I think I see the problem," said the doctor. "You haven't been eating any greens."

Stripes or Solids

A monkey and a zebra prepare to play pool. The zebra says, "I call stripes!"

Pool Quips

I tossed my billiard table into the bathtub. Now I have a swimming pool.

I hinted to my friend that if he wanted to improve his billiards game, he should get better equipment. . .unfortunately, he took my cue.

Riddle Roundup

What is green and fuzzy with four legs—and would kill you if it landed on you?
A billiards table.

Why do elephants wear green shoes?
So they can sneak across pool tables.

Have you ever seen an elephant sneaking across a pool table?
Works, doesn't it?

RACING

Of course, they didn't have cars in Bible times. But some people drove chariots, and it was said of a guy named Jehu that "he drives like a maniac" (2 Kings 9:20). He was just about three thousand years too early for NASCAR.

....

Knock, Knock

Knock, knock.
Who's there?
Cargo.
Cargo who?
Cargo better if you fill the tank with gas.

Knock, knock.
Who's there?
Phillip.
Phillip who?
Phillip my car with gas. It's going to be a long race!

Riddle Roundup

Why are penguins good race drivers?
Because they're always in the pole position!

What did the tornado say to the sports car?
Want to go for a spin?

Why don't race car drivers eat a lot before a race?
They don't want to get indy-gestion.

What did the race car driver say after another driver crashed into him?
"Give me a brake!"

What did the crew chief say to the mechanic who didn't put the tire on the car properly?
"That's nuts!"

RUNNING, TRACK, AND FIELD EVENTS

Do you like to run? Some people love it, others loathe it. . .but the Bible uses running as a picture for all of life: "Let us run with perseverance the race marked out for us" (Hebrews 12:1). Now, run through these jokes to see which ones win the prize:

....

Cross Country

You might be a cross country runner if. . .

- Your toenails are black.
- Your shoes have more miles on them than your car does.
- People say, "You run three miles—all at one time?"
- You run farther in a week than your bus travels for meets.
- The most enjoyable time you've had all month is a day off from practice.
- You can spit and run at the same time.
- You can eat your weight in spaghetti.
- You eat spaghetti three times a day.
- You schedule activities around meets.

- You wake up every morning in pain.
- Your Saturdays for the next four years are ruined.
- You can see your ribs through your shirt.
- You have to run around in the shower to get wet.
- Your dessert is Brussels sprouts.

A Limerick

A javelin thrower called Vicky,
Found the grip of her javelin sticky.
When it came to the throw;
She couldn't let go;
Making judging the distance quite tricky.

Knock, Knock

Knock, knock.
  Who's there?
Hydrate.
  Hydrate who?
Hydrate you at least a nine out of ten!

Knock, knock.
  Who's there?
Eyesore.
  Eyesore who?

Eyesore from running. Can we take the elevator?

What's the Time?

A young man set out on a trip across the country to visit his family for Christmas. He drove all night and knew he needed to stop to sleep because he was getting tired. He found what he thought was a quiet place to get a nap, next to a tree-lined jogging path. He had just drifted off to sleep when he was awakened by a knock on his window. "Excuse me," a young woman called. "Do you happen to have the time?"

The man peered at watch and said, "Yeah, it's 7:03."

"Thank you," the jogger said cheerfully, and left with a wave.

The driver settled back into his seat and drifted off to sleep again. A few moments later, there was another knock at his window.

"I'm sorry to bother you," another jogger said. "But can you please tell me what time it is?"

A bit annoyed, the young man answered, "Yes, it's 7:10."

"Thanks!" the jogger replied, then turned

and continued on his way.

The worn-out driver realized that other runners might stop too, so he found a piece of paper and wrote, "I do not know what time it is," and posted it in his window. Then he closed his eyes and snuggled down to sleep.

A few minutes later, there was a tap on his window.

Startled, the driver opened his eyes to see yet another jogger. His patience gone, he called, "I don't know the time!"

"I know!" the jogger said. "I just wanted you to let you know that it's 7:18."

Someone Else's Shoes

Before you criticize someone, you should walk a mile in their shoes. So when you criticize them, you have a mile between you, plus, you have their shoes!

Meter Check

Two workers were checking gas meters in a neighborhood after someone had called to report the smell of natural gas in the area. They were working from one house to the next, using their equipment to detect any signs of a leak.

Toward the end of the day, they were getting tired. "After we check this one, let's have a race down the driveway. Loser buys the other one a candy bar of their choice."

"You've got a deal!" the other worker exclaimed.

After another negative reading, the workers took off down the driveway as fast as they could. When they reached the sidewalk, they were surprised a woman was running after them, gasping for breath.

"Uh, ma'am, is everything okay?" asked a worker.

"I don't know—you tell me!" she said, gasping. "When I saw you two servicing the gas meter outside my window and take off running, I figured that I'd better run too!"

Riddle Roundup

Why did the pig have to quit the race?
  He pulled his hamstring.

How do you start a firefly race?
  Ready, set, glow!

Why did the bald Englishman take up running?
  To get some fresh 'air.

Why do elephants wear running shoes?
For running, of course.

Did you hear about the two silkworms' race?
It ended in a tie.

Why did the hamburger always lose the race?
It could never ketchup.

Did you hear about the lazy athlete?
He came in fourth so that he wouldn't have to walk up to the podium.

What is the difference between a sprinter and a locomotive engineer?
One is trained to run, the other runs a train.

A carrot and lettuce raced each other.
Who won?
The lettuce. At the finish line, it was the one that was a head.

Who is the all-time fastest runner?
Adam, because he was first in the human race.

What happens when you run behind a car?
You get exhausted.

If runners get athlete's foot, what do astronauts get?

Mistletoe.

Why did the vegetarian quit the cross-country team?

He didn't like the meets.

How did the barber win the race?

He took a short cut.

SKATING

Everyone knows Jesus once walked on water. Skaters (and the rest of us) can only do that when the water is frozen.

....

The Cutting Edge

Q: How is music like ice skating?
A: If you don't "C sharp," you'll "B flat."

Injury Treatment

While ice skating, Bob took a nasty fall. The rink doctor rushed out to examine him but decided there was little he could do for the large bruise on Bob's forehead. All he could suggest was, "Would you like some ice?"

Judge This!

The Olympic men's figure skating competition begins with a Russian competitor. His costume is a little on the drab side, and he skates to a very serious classical music soundtrack. The skater is strong at his leaps

but lacks the flair of previous Russian
competitors. The judges show their scores:

> Britain: 5.8
> Russia: 5.9
> United States: 5.7
> South Slobobia: 6.0

Next up is an American skater, who boogies
to an upbeat rock-and-roll tune, flashing by
in a sparkly stars-and-stripes costume. Tech-
nically, he's not quite as good as the Russian,
but the fans are more excited by his performance. The judges show their scores:

> Britain: 5.8
> Russia: 5.7
> United States: 5.9
> South Slobobia: 6.0

Finally, the South Slobobian competitor steps
onto the ice, and immediately falls down face
first. Nose bleeding, he gets back up and falls
down again. This happens over and over until
he finally crawls off the ice. The crowd waits
in embarrassed silence until the judges show
their scores:

Britain: 0.0
Russia: 0.0
United States: 0.0
South Slobobia: 6.0

The other three judges are shocked, and turn to the South Slobobian judge to demand, "How could you give that awful performance a 6.0?"

"Hey," the judge replies. "You've got to remember—it's slippery out there!"

Signs You're Not a Perfect 6.0

- Judges can't tell the difference between you and the Zamboni.
- Your coach is yelling, "Let go of the railing!"
- You Lutz yourself over the boards and into a hot dog vendor.
- During a spin, your skate flies off and embeds itself in the judge's arm.
- You cut your program short because you have to return your rental skates.

Riddle Roundup

What is the hardest thing about learning to skate?

The ice.

What is the hardest thing about learning to roller skate?

The floor.

Why shouldn't you tell a joke while you are ice skating?

Because the ice might crack up.

SKIING

It's tough to make any connections with skiing in the Bible. But today, there's a ski resort on the biblical Mount Hermon. Wanna go?

....

Riddle Roundup

Where does a skier cash his checks?
At a snow bank.

What do you call a slow skier?
A slope-poke.

How does a skier get to school?
By icicle.

Why should you invite a skier to Thanksgiving dinner?
Because they're good at carving.

What do skiers eat for breakfast?
Frosted Flakes.

What do you get when you cross a skier with a vampire?
Frostbite.

How do skiers correct their mistakes?
With whiteout.

Why did the skier expect the worst when she reached the top of the hill?
She knew it was all downhill from there.

What do skiers eat for lunch?
Icebergers.

What do skiers like most about school?
Snow and tell.

Why shouldn't you spend too much time on a chair lift?
It just isn't nice to always be looking down on people.

What kind of cakes do skiers like best?
Ones with thick icing.

SOCCER

Normally, we tell children not to run around and kick things. But, somehow, in soccer it's okay. What about that verse that says, "start children off on the way they should go. . ." (Proverbs 22:6)?

....

Soccer Quips

Millions of people play soccer because that way they don't have to watch it on television.

Soccer players do better in school than football players because soccer players use their heads.

I don't play soccer because I enjoy the sport. I just do it for the kicks.

Q & A

Q: What has twenty-two legs and says, "Crunch, crunch, crunch"?
A: A soccer team eating potato chips.

Q: What position did Dracula play on his soccer team?
A: Ghoulie.

Q: What were the soccer star's first words as a baby?
A: "Look, Mom, no hands."

Q: Why do soccer players have so much trouble eating popcorn?
A: They think they can't use their hands.

Q: Why is Cinderella not a good soccer player?
A: She's always running away from the ball.

Q: When it gets dark, how do they light up a soccer stadium?
A: With a soccer match.

Slippery When Wet

A mom had just finished washing the kitchen floor when she heard her son open the front door. "Be careful on the floor, Conner!" she shouted. "I don't want you to slip. I just washed it."

"That's okay, Mom," Conner said, stepping onto the floor. "I'm wearing my cleats."

Jungle Game

It was a boring afternoon in the jungle, so the elephants decided to challenge the ants to a game of soccer. The game was going well, with the elephants beating the ants ten goals to zip, when the ants gained possession.

The ants' star player was advancing the ball toward the elephants' goal when the elephants' left back came lumbering toward him. The elephant stepped on the little ant, killing him instantly.

The referee stopped the game. "What do you think you're doing? Do you call that sportsmanship, killing another player?"

The elephant sadly replied, "I didn't mean to kill him—I was just trying to trip him up."

Know-It-All

Coach: So you think you know everything there is to know about soccer?
New player: Yes, Coach. I do. I've played so long, there's nothing I don't know about it.
Coach: Oh, really? Well then, how many holes are in the net?

No Game

In a far-off eastern country, the game of soccer was the most popular sport. Everybody played it, even the royal family. But one day, the king died, and a new king took his place. The new king hated soccer and outlawed it, so all the games had to be abandoned. You could say *reign* stopped play.

Heckler

The crowd was mercilessly jeering and heckling the referee in a high school match. Finally, the poor official walked over to the bleachers and sat down next to his loudest critic.

"What are you doing?" asked the spectator.

"Well," said the ref, "it seems you get the best view from here."

Riddle Roundup

What game do girls dislike?
Soccer [sock her].

Which goalkeeper can jump higher than a crossbar?
All of them. A crossbar can't jump!

Why are soccer players never asked out to dinner?

Because they're always dribbling.

SWIMMING

You remember the great Bible swimmer Jonah, right? Well, maybe he wasn't such a great swimmer after all. He sank like a stone, right into the mouth of that big fish. . . .

....

Knock, Knock

Knock, knock.
Who's there?
Dwayne.
Dwayne who?
Dwayne de pool, I'm dwowning!

Knock, knock.
Who's there?
Thatcher.
Thatcher who?
Thatcher idea of a dive?

Q & A

Q: Why do you keep doing the backstroke?
A: I've just had lunch, and I don't want to swim on a full stomach.

Taking a Dip

I took a dip in the hotel pool. The lifeguard asked, "What have you got there?"

"Nacho cheese," I said.

Donation

A woman knocked on my door today, asking for a small donation for the local pool.

I gave her a glass of water.

Fun at a Swimming Pool

- Stand on top of the high dive and say you won't come down until your demands are met.
- Ask people if they've seen your pet shark.
- Play Marco Polo by yourself.

Swimming Pondering

If one synchronized swimmer drowns, do the rest have to drown too?

Race of His Life

A very rich man loved alligators, and, for a party he was hosting at his sprawling estate, had four of them added to his swimming pool. His guests were amazed by the exotic animals.

Dusk fell, and the lights illuminated the pool and surrounding area. The party host got his guests' attention and announced, "If anyone can swim from one end of the pool to the other, I will buy them a new car." Some guests looked as if they were considering the offer, but no one made a move. Suddenly, there was a splash. They all watched in amazement as a man swam at high speed from one end of the pool to the other. He jumped out, unharmed.

The host was astonished. "I absolutely cannot believe you took me up on that!" he exclaimed. "I was really joking, but I'm a man of my word. What kind of car do you want?"

"Car?" shouted the man. "I don't care about a car! I just want to know who it was that pushed me into the pool!"

Pool Game

What game do chickens play in the pool?
Marco Pollo.

Swim Delay

Jimmy: You wanted to go swimming, didn't you?

Kent: Yes.

Jimmy: Well, water you waiting for?

Nonswimmer

Elmer: Waiter, waiter! There's a dead fly swimming in my soup.

Waiter: Nonsense, sir. Dead flies can't swim.

No Diving

A man in a swimming pool was on the very top diving board. He poised, lifted his arms, and was about to dive when the attendant came running up, shouting, "Don't dive! There's no water in that pool."

"That's all right," said the man. "I can't swim."

Keep an Eye

"I thought I told you to keep an eye on your cousin," the mother impatiently barked. "Where is he?"

"Well," her son replied thoughtfully, "if he

knows as much about canoeing as he thinks he does, he's out canoeing. If he knows as little as I think he does, he's out swimming."

Riddle Roundup

Is it dangerous to swim on a full stomach?
  Yes. It is better to swim in water.

How do swimmers get to work?
  They car pool.

Why did the lifeguard throw the elephants out of the swimming pool?
  Because they couldn't keep their trunks up.

Why did the cantaloupe dive into the pool?
  It wanted to be a watermelon.

Why shouldn't you listen to people who have just come out of the swimming pool?
  Because they are all wet.

What would you get if you crossed a movie house and a swimming pool?
  A dive-in theater.

What kind of poles can swim?
  Tadpoles.

TENNIS

People like to say you can find *tennis* in the Bible, when Joseph served in Pharaoh's court. Ha ha!

....

Brutal Honesty

Ella: I just adore tennis. I could play like this forever.

Curtis: You will, if you don't take lessons.

Sign Here, Please

Tennis champs are getting so young they give autographs in crayon.

Tennis Q & A

Q: What did one tennis ball say to the other tennis ball?

A: See you 'round.

Q: What's a horse's favorite sport?

A: Stable tennis.

Q: What sport do waiters do the best at?

A: Tennis, because they serve well.

Tennis Ponderings

Never marry a tennis player, because to him love means nothing.

Knock, Knock

Knock, knock.
>   *Who's there?*

Tennis!
>   *Tennis who?*

Tennis five plus five.

Riddle Roundup

What is the loudest sport?
>   *Tennis, because everyone raises a racket.*

What can you serve but never eat?
>   *A tennis ball.*

Where do tennis players go on a date?
>   *The Tennis Ball.*

Which state has the most tennis players?
>   *Tennis-ee.*

Why are fish not good tennis players?
>   *They don't like getting near the net.*

How can you tell if a tennis player doesn't like your serve?

They keep returning it.

How many tennis players does it take to change a light bulb?

Only one, but they need to admit that it's out.

What is a tennis player's bedtime?

Tennish.

VOLLEYBALL

People like to say you can find *volleyball* in the Bible, when Joseph served in Pharaoh's court. Ha ha again!

....

Riddle Roundup

How are a carpenter and a volleyball player alike?
They both like to hammer spikes.

What does a police officer do on a volleyball court?
Serve and protect.

What can be served but never eaten?
A volleyball.

What do you call a girl who is standing in the middle of the volleyball court?
Annette.

Why do volleyball players want to join the armed forces?
So they can get experience in the service.

WEIGHTLIFTING

Samson is the Bible's weightlifter.
Ever heard this story? "He got up and
took hold of the doors of the city gate,
together with the two posts, and tore them
loose, bar and all. He lifted them to his
shoulders and carried them to the top of
the hill that faces Hebron" (Judges 16:3).
Whew, look at those muscles!

....

Heavy Weights

A dad was skeptical of his son's newfound
determination to work out, but he took the
teenager to the sporting goods store to look
at weight sets. "Please, Dad," begged the boy,
"I promise I will use them every day."

"I just don't know, Will. It's a huge com-
mitment," the father told him.

"I know, Dad," the boy replied.

"They're not cheap, either," his dad
continued.

"I'll use them, I promise! You'll see."

Finally agreeing to make the purchase,
the father paid for the equipment, and they
started for the door.

"Here, son," said the dad. "You carry the
weights."

Will whimpered, "You mean I have to carry them all the way to the car?"

Protein Purchase

A weightlifter went into a health food store and asked for a large container of protein.

"I'm sorry, we're all out," said the store employee.

"What!" said the weightlifter. "No whey!"

Business Trip

Courtney was making arrangements for a business trip. She hoped to find a hotel with exercise facilities but had to make the reservation without talking to anyone directly.

The time came for the trip, and Courtney flew to the destination. After a long day of travel, she wearily walked to the front desk and checked in to the hotel. When the desk clerk asked if she had any additional questions, she said, "Just one. Which way to your weight room?"

"Oh, we don't have a weight room," he replied. "But we have a very nice lobby, and you're welcome to wait there."

Membership

I wanted to sign up for a gym membership so that I could start weightlifting. The desk attendant told me it was $150 a year. I declined, because I thought that was too much for one visit.

Confession

After two weeks of keeping it secret, I confessed to my friend that I had taken the bench press out of my workout schedule. That was a huge weight off my chest.

Dropping Weight

I started going to the gym and I dropped weight really quickly. I'm so thankful those dumbbells missed my feet!

Riddle Roundup

Have you heard the best weightlifting joke?
You'll have to weight for it.

Did you hear about the vegetable who lifts weights?
He is a muscle sprout.

What exercise to hairdressers do in the gym?
    Curls.

Why do impatient people avoid the gym?
    Because of the weights.

Why was the weightlifter sad after lifting the case of cola?
    It was soda pressing.

Why did the clam stop lifting weights?
    He pulled a mussel.

What does a weightlifter do to build muscle?
    Lift weights.

What does a weightlifter do for cardio?
    Lift weights really fast.

Did you hear about the weightlifter who was asked to leave the gym?
    He was doing diddly squats.

OTHER SPORTS AND LEISURE JOKES

Whatever your favorite sport or game, be sure to thank God for it. He "richly provides us with everything for our enjoyment" (1 Timothy 6:17).

....

Chess Players

A group of chess enthusiasts checked into a hotel and were standing in the lobby discussing their recent tournament victories. After an hour, the manager came out of the office and asked them to disperse.

"But why?" they asked as they moved off.

"Because," the manager explained, "I can't stand chess nuts boastin' in an open foyer."

Chess Q & A

Q: What's the difference between a chess player and a man who is broke?

A: One watches his pawns; the other pawns his watch.

Skydiving

If at first you don't succeed,
skydiving is definitely not for you.

Seasons

Teacher: Name the four seasons.
Athlete: Baseball, basketball, football, and
   hockey.

Swing on This

Chuck: Did you hear about the trapeze per-
   former who fell to the ground?
Buck: Did he hit a net first?
Chuck: Yes, and Annette wasn't too happy
   about it.

Time on Your Hands

"I bet I can run faster than you can," bragged
Hank to Frank.

"I bet you can't," replied Frank.

To prove his point, Hank took Frank to the
roof of a thirty-story building. Hank removed
his watch and dropped it over the edge of
the building. Quickly, in a whirl of dust, Hank
dashed down the stairs. Reaching the ground

floor, he reached out his hand and caught the watch.

Signaling it was his turn, Frank removed his watch and let it fall. Taking his time, he strolled to the elevator and pushed the button. A few minutes later, the elevator appeared and Frank stepped in. After stopping at several floors, he arrived at the lobby, stepped out, and calmly walked outdoors just in time to put out a hand and catch his watch.

"Hey, that was amazing!" remarked Hank. "How did you do it?"

"Simple," said Frank. "My watch is five minutes slow."

Chess One-Liner

I had lunch with a chess champion the other day. It took him fifteen minutes to pass the salt.

Poor Grandpa

Cindy: I can't believe you took your blind grandfather skydiving.
Mindy: He really enjoyed it.
Cindy: Do you plan to do it again?
Mindy: No way.
Cindy: But he liked it. Why not?

Mindy: Well, he enjoyed it, but his guide dog wasn't too crazy about it.

Varsity IQ

Did you hear about the athlete who was so *dumb* that when he earned his varsity letter, someone had to read it to him?

Observation

A small girl watching a water skier said, "That man is so silly. He'll never catch that boat."

Good News and Bad News

A college crew team had spent the whole afternoon rowing and they were exhausted. Heading for the locker room, their coach stopped them. "I have some good news and some bad news," he said. "The good news is that you can take a fifteen-minute break and then the college president is coming down here to watch you row."

There was a groan throughout the team. One rower asked, "If that's the good news, what's the bad news?"

"Well," the coach answered, "he's bringing his water skis."

Bad Skydiving

Alfred is a daredevil, so he decides to go sky-diving for the very first time. After listening to the instructor for what seems like days, he is ready to go.

Excited, he jumps out of the airplane. About five seconds later, he pulls the ripcord. Nothing happens. He tries again. Still nothing. Alfred starts to panic, but remembers his backup chute. He pulls that cord. Nothing happens. He frantically begins pulling both cords, but to no avail.

Suddenly, he looks down, and he can't believe his eyes. Another man is in the air with him, but this guy is going up! Just as the other guy passes by, the totally scared Alfred yells, "Hey, do you know anything about skydiving?"

The other man yells back, "Are you kidding? Do you know anything about lighting gas stoves?"

Parachute Instructions

Parachute recall notice: On page 6 of the instruction manual, please change the words "state zip code" to "pull rip cord."

Seat Location

On her way back from the concession stand, Julie asked a man at the end of the row, "Pardon me, but did I step on your foot a few minutes ago?"

Expecting an apology, the man said, "Indeed you did."

Julie nodded and noted, "Oh, good. Then this is my row."

Halftime Entertainment

The band had just finished its under-rehearsed selection and received a big ovation from the stands. A woman in the front row stood up and shouted, "Play it again! Play it again!" The band director and drum majors all bowed directly to the woman. Then she yelled, "Play it again until you get it right!"

Sports Medicine

A burly professional wrestler was sitting in a doctor's office and kept mumbling, "I hope I'm sick, I hope I'm sick." Another waiting patient asked why he wanted to be sick. The wrestler replied, "I'd hate to be well and feel like this."

The college jock sat on his doctor's examination table explaining the pain in his arm. The doctor asked, "Did you ever have this before?" The young athlete admitted that he did, to which the doctor answered, "Well, you've got it again."

Foresight

Luke: I think sports are boring.
Lisa: Why do you think that?
Luke: I can tell you the score before the game even begins.
Lisa: Really?
Luke: Yup. It's 0 to 0.

Sword Swallowing

Did you hear about the sword swallower who swallowed an umbrella? He wanted to put something away for a rainy day.

Skydiving Risk

Reporter: Why are you a skydiver? Isn't it extremely dangerous jumping out of airplanes?
Skydiver: No, jumping out is a piece of cake. But it does get riskier as you approach the ground.

Playing Fair

A mother scolded her son for not being fair with his little brother. "You need to give him a turn with your skateboard," she told him.

"Mom, I have," he said. "I ride it down the hill, and he gets to ride it back up to the top."

Where Did He Go?

I signed up for the hide-and-seek championship. I forgot all about it and won first prize.

Yep

I wanted to organize a professional hide-and-seek tournament, but it has been quite difficult. Good players are hard to find.

Name Confusion

Mr. and Mrs. Jackson had two children. One was named Mind Your Own Business and the other was named Trouble.

One day the kids decided to play hide-and-seek. Trouble hid while Mind Your Own Business counted to fifty. Mind Your Own Business began looking for her brother all over the house. When he couldn't be found, she looked in the garage, then moved outside to the yard, Still not finding him, she moved down the block, looking behind garbage cans and in bushes. She had just begun looking under cards when a police officer approached her and asked, "What are you doing?"

"Playing a game," the girl replied.

"What is your name?" the officer asked.

"Mind Your Own Business."

The police officer did not care for this disrespect and asked the youngster, "Are you looking for trouble?"

The girl, startled by his question, admitted, "Why, yes I am!"

Riddle Roundup

What season is it when you are on a trampoline?
Springtime.

Why did the tightrope walker always carry his bankbook?
So he could check his balance.

What game do you play in water?
Swimming pool.

How can you go surfing in the kitchen?
On a microwave.

What do you call a boomerang that doesn't work?

A stick.

What is a toad's favorite game?

Leapfrog.

What is a frog's favorite exercise?

Jumping jacks.

Where is a dog's favorite place to hide during hide-and-seek?

Roof.

Why shouldn't you play hide-and-seek with mountains?

Because they just can't help peaking.

What is a mathematician's favorite recess game?

Four squared.

Why are dalmatians bad at hide-and-seek?

They're always spotted.

Which classical composer is best at playing hide-and-seek?

Haydn.

What do you call four bullfighters in quicksand?

Quattro sinko.

What is a mosquito's favorite sport?

Skindiving.

What is an elephant's favorite sport?

Squash.

What is a zucchini's favorite game?

Squash.

How many people can you fit into an empty sports stadium?

One. After that it's not empty.

Do Eskimos go on safaris?

Not safaris I know.

What is the hardest part of skydiving?

The ground.

What is the best mountain to climb to get a good night's sleep?

Mount Ever-rest.

How did the T-Rex feel after his workout?

Dinos-sore.

Why did the boys fire their BB guns into the air?
They liked to shoot the breeze.

What is the noisiest sport?
Racket ball.

Why did the dancer quit ballet?
Because it was tu-tu difficult.

MORE GREAT JOKES FOR KIDS!

This hilarious collection of jokes, funny stories, riddles, and one-liners is sure to make anyone laugh. . .even you sourpusses! Perfect for 8–12-year-olds, *An Arkful of Animal Jokes— for Kids!* features chapters on more than 30 kinds of animals, from alligators to chickens, monkeys to skunkies, and snails to zebras.

Paperback / 978-1-64352-251-7 / $4.99

COMING SOON FROM SHILOH KIDZ!

(Coming September 2020)

Would you rather. . .
Be bombed with giant hailstones? (Joshua 10:1-11)
OR
Be chased from your hometown by swarms of angry hornets? (Joshua 24:11-13)

This fun, interactive devotional journal and sketchbook for the adventurous kids will keep them entertained while they learn about some of the weird, gross, and unbelievable stories found in the Bible.

Dozens of Bible story-based devotions alongside wonderfully unexpected, "Would You Rather. . .?" journal prompts and sketch pages will help kids dig deeper into their Bibles, as they learn that God's Word is never boring and always applies to everyday life!

Spiral Bound / 978-1-64352-557-0 / $12.99